CULINARY HISTORY OF THE GANGETIC PLAINS

THE FOOD BOWL BETWEEN INDUS AND BRAHMAPUTRA DELTAS

DR ANSHUMALI PANDEY

Contents

Foreword

The world population has grown by about five billion since the beginning of the Green Revolution and many believe that, without the Revolution, there would have been greater famine and malnutrition. Population movements increase urban populations and reduce rural populations. This reduces labor productivity in agricultural areas and causes these areas to remain inactive and increases the pressure of urban development on these areas. Keeping above in view the I present this book "Culinary History of the Gangetic Plains" has been attempted.

Agriculture is extremely important as it not only provides food and a sense of livelihood to many people in India, but also is a source of employment for many. Being a relatively poorer in certain parts of India, the jobs created as a result of agriculture contribute majorly to people's incomes and livelihoods. As a result, agricultural industries greatly add to the Gross Domestic Product of India and consequently lead to benefits to the economy such as an increased multiplier effect.

Historically, the civilizations established on fertile lands with assure supply of water for livelihood as well as for crops and animals. In India too Indo Gangetic plains bestowed with fertile land as well as adequate supply and availability of water for humans and animals; and irrigation purposes. Therefore, as expected in past history the population density increased more in the Indo Gangetic Plains due to favorable soils and water availability.

Dr Anshumali Pandey

Preface

Indo-Gangetic Plain, also called North Indian Plain, extensive north-central section of the Indian subcontinent, stretching westward from (and including) the combined delta of the Brahmaputra River valley and the Ganges (Ganga) River to the Indus River valley.

CHAPTER ONE

The Indo Gangetic Plains

History of Indo Gangetic Plains:

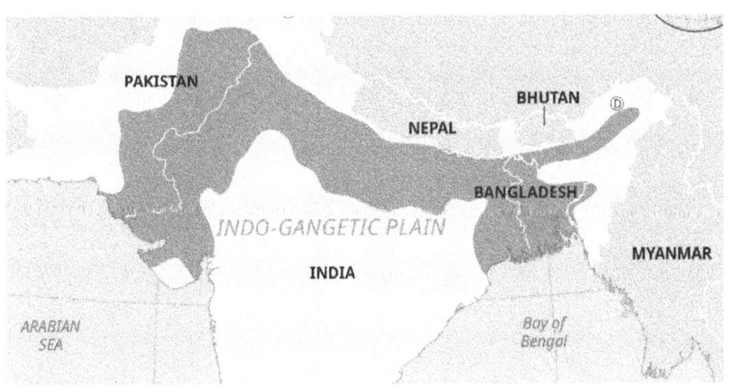

Indo-Gangetic Plain, also known as the North Indus Plain, stretches to the west (including) from the Brahmaputra River Valley and Ganges (Ganga), to the Indus River Valley, from the North Indian Plain, a large north-central portion of the Indian subsoil region. The region includes affluent and most populated regions of the subcontinent. Most of the plain is comprised of alluvial soil formed by the three major rivers

and their tributaries. Weak rainfall or drought in winter arise in the eastern portion of the region, but in the summer rainfall are so extreme that large areas become swamps or freshwater lakes. The plain eventually dries to the west where the Thar Desert incorporated.

The Indo-Gangetic Plains are found in the states of Punjab, Haryana, Uttar Pradesh, Bihar and West Bengal and consist of two major drainage basins: the drainage basin Punjab and Haryana, and the drainage basin Ganges-Brahmaputra. The entire Plain is between 400-800 km wide and is now a sinking basin due to seismic changes in the earth. The land is highly fertile due to the nature of the Indo-Gangetic Plains, and is thus suitable for farming activities.

Delhi, Lucknow and Chandigarh are some notable cities situated here. These regions are considered among the most extensively farmed in the whole world, consisting mostly of wheat and rice cultivation. Some other traditional crops are also found in these regions, however, such as cotton, corn, and sugarcane. The region has an incredibly high population density as a result of this expanded cultivation and almost one hundred crore people actually live here.

Dividing the entire area into 5 separate sub-regions. Regions 1 and 2 are spread around Pakistan, Haryana and Punjab, Regions 3 and 4 inhabit Uttar Pradesh, Bihar and Nepal and lastly West Bengal and Bangladesh constitutes of Region 5. The Indo-Gangetic Plains prime area means that the temperature varies from dry to mild climates. This means the city is having mild, humid, rainy summers and cold, dry winters. Monsoon rains which occur in this region most directly affect the climate.

Indus-Ganga Plains are large floodplains of the Indus, Ganga and Brahmaputra River System and are also known as the "Great Plains". They pass from Jammu and Kashmir and Khyber Pakhtunkhwa, in the west and Assam in the east, paralleling the Himalayas and draining almost all of north and east India. The plains occupy an area of Seven Lakh Square Kilometers and vary from several hundred kilometers wide in their range. The Ganges and the Indus rivers are the main rivers in this system and their affluent rivers includes Beas, Yamuna, Gomti, Ravi, Khambale, Sutlej and Chenab. The Indus-Ganga belt is the largest contiguous alluvial expanse in the world created by the silt deposits of many rivers. The plains are level and largely treeless, and can be irrigated by canals. The region is also rich in supplies of freshwater. The plains are the most heavily agricultural regions in the country. The major crops planted are rice and wheat which grown in rotation. The corn, sugarcane and cotton are also some of them. With a population estimate reaching 40 Crore, the Indo-Gangetic plains are among the most heavily inhabited regions of the planet.

Natural Resources of Indo Gangetic Plains:

The Central Research Institute for Dry Agriculture (CRIDA) prepared the NRI (Natural Resource Index) map of India to the National Rain-fed Region Authority (NRAA) for Seven factors i.e. rainfall, status of groundwater, irrigation intensity, rainfed area, drought, available water content of the soil, degraded land area and waste lands. Two thirds of the allocated size are accounted for by the

NRI; rainfall and drought represent the biggest share of the NRI as the consequence of rainfed agriculture is calculated. The map shows that the eastern part of the country is resource-rich, middle part (split vertically) is medium-rich and the western part is relatively poor.

This is the large unit in the Great Plain of India, occupying an area of approximately 3.75 lakh sq km, from Delhi to Kolkata in Uttar Pradesh, Bihar and West Bengal. The Ganga is the major river because of this the plain name is named as Indo Gangetic Plains. The Ganga and its huge number of affluent in the Himalayas-the Yamuna, Gomati, Ghaghara, Gandak, Kosi, etc. carried from the mountains massive volumes of alluvium and dumped it there in order to create this vast plain. Also contributing to the development of this plain were the peninsula 's banks such as Chambal, Betwa, Ken, Son, etc. The general slope of the entire plain is to the east and south east.

This plain can be further divided into the following three sections based on its geographical variations:

(a) The Upper Ganga Plain.

(b) The Middle Ganga Plain.

(c) The Lower Ganga Plain.

(a) The Upper Ganga Plain: This plain occupies the upper part of the Ganga Plain and is bound in the north by the 300m Shivaliks, and in the south by the Peninsula, and in the west by the Yamuna River. The eastern boundary is very mysterious, and among geographers it has become a controversial theme. The plain is approximately 550 km east-west and approximately 380 km North-South covering an area of approximately 1.49 lakh sq km in length. Its height ranges from 100 to 300 m above sea level. The Ganga and as well as the Yamuna, Ram Ganga, Sarda, Gomati and Ghaghara are flooding the plains. Nearly all of the rivers flow through NW-SE with the lie of the land. The land slope is around 25 cm per km on average. In the northern portion, the gradient is comparatively steep. If the elevation rises, the rivers rise steadily throughout the plain. his flat and unusual plain is occupied by the submontane of Tarai-Bhabar and the bluffs of the river, river meanders and oxbow lakes, levees, abandoned river courses, sandy stretches (Bhurs) and the river canals themselves. This flat and unusual plain is rendered monotonous. The west portion of the plane consists of Ganga-Yamuna Doab which is moderately higher. The low-lying Rohilkhand plains unite to the east of the doab into the Avadh plains. The Avadh plains largest river is Ghaghara. The khadar of this river's is very high, as the river is passing through this area. It often changes its direction regularly.

(b) The Middle Ganga Plain: To the east of the Upper Ganga plain is Middle Ganga plain occupying eastern part of Uttar Pradesh and Bihar. It spans roughly 600 km east-west and approximately 330 km north-south, creating a combined area of approximately 1.44 lakh sq km. Its northern and southern boundaries are well defined by the Himalayan foothills and the Peninsular edge respectively. Its western and eastern frontiers were very unclear, and both sides of the Ganga plain had a large area, which gave it the character of the eastern-west continuum. There is no physical limit worthy of this name, and the plain opens up from the upper Ganga plain to the west imperceptibly and dies almost invisibly into the lower Ganga plain to the east. As such, the Ganga Valley represents a transformation area par excellence. However, there are many attempts to demarcate these intermediate zones of western and eastern boundaries. These boundaries are more widely accepted by 100 m in the west, 75 m in the north-east, and 30 m in the south-east. This is clearly a very low plain, not more than 150 m in elevation. The Ghaghara, the Gandak, the Kosi and all the Ganga tributaries that come from the Himalayas drain this plain. These rivers fill the alluvial deposits at the foot of the Nepal Himalayas with 2.000 m deep troughs. They steadily pass across this flat land which has marked the region with local landmarks like levees, bluffs, oxbow reservoirs, marshlands, valleys, ravines and so on. The composition of the Kankar is relatively limited because of the khadar supremacy. Nearly every river continues to travel its routes and this region is vulnerable to regular flooding. In this sense, the Kosi River is very popular. In 1736, it flowed in the vicinity of Purnea, and now it is roughly 110 km west. Occasionally, in 24 hours the water level has raised by 10 metres. The 'Sorrow of Bihar' has long been renamed. This river is being tame by intense efforts both by India and Nepal. Ganga-Ghaghara doab, Ghaghara-GandakDoab and Gandak-Kosi Doab (the plain of Mithila) are the most important elements in this plain. The Son is the most important, with some rivers joining the Ganga from the south. . Here, in the east of Uttar Pradesh, the gradient is steeper than the 9-10 cm per km and in the Mithila plain just 6 cm per km. The Magadh Plain is to the east of Son River.

(c) **The Lower Ganga Plain:** The Purnea district of Bihar, the whole West of Bengal (excluding Purulia District and Darjeeling Mountain Parts) and much of Bangladesh are located in this area. It is approximately 580 kilometres away in the north from Darjeeling Himalaya to Bay of Bengal in the south, and approximately 200 kilometres from the Chotanagpur mountains on the western frontier to Bangladesh in the East. This plain consists of about 81,000 sq km of total area. His width varies considerably, and it is just 16 km from Bangladesh to Rajmahal Hills. The outline of 50 m is nearly the western edge. The sediment deposited by Tista, Jaldhaka and Torsa formed the northern part of this plain. In addition, the Duars (Darjeeling Tarai) and the plain of Barindcharacterise this region, the ancient alluvium tract between the Kosi-Mahananda corridor in the west and the Sankosh river in the east. About two thirds of the plain are in the shape of the Delta. It is the world's greatest delta. In the delta zone, the Ganga River breaks into many channels. The slope of land is just 2 cm per km. The surface area is 2/3 below the normal sea level of 30 m. If the sea level raised by just seven feet, the entire land up to Kolkata will be fully submerged. A broad variety of estuaries, mud flats, mangrove wetlands, sandbanks, beaches and forelands lies down against the seafront of the delta. The coastal delta is protected in a large part by massive, impenetrable tidal forests. The Sunderbans are named because here the Sundri tree is prevalent.

Punjab – The Land of Five Rivers

Punjab, the land of the five rivers-Beas, Satluj, Chenab, Ravi and Jhelum, is also called the land of milk and honey. Perhaps it would be appropriate to call it the land of plenty.

"*Punjabi cooking and eating is just like the Punjabis themselves. It is simple and forthright. Punjabis are a hardworking and fun loving community by nature with food and merriment, very much a part of their lives. Punjabi cuisine has always been strongly influenced by Mughal invaders who brought with them the tradition of the great Tandoor and now Punjabi Tandoori cooking is celebrated as one of the most popular cuisine throughout the world.*"

GEOGRAPHY:

Punjab is located in the northwest of India having international border with Pakistan on the western side. River Satluj and Ravi flow along most parts of this international border. It is bordered by the Indian states of Jammu and Kashmir on the north, Himachal Pradesh on its northeast and Haryana and Rajasthan to its south. On the map, it is triangular in shape. Pathankot district is at the top of the triangle; Fazilka and Patiala are respectively at the bottom left and right corners of this triangular shape. It covers a geographical area of 50,362 sq. km which is 1.54 % of country's total geographical area. Punjab state is located between 29° 30' N to 32° 32' N latitude and between 73° 55' E to 76° 50' E longitude. Its average elevation is 300 m from the sea level.

The state of Punjab is situated in the Indo-Gangetic alluvial plains, also called as Great Plains. Most of the land of Punjab is an alluvial plain formed by the sedimentation deposited by many rivers and canals flowing through this land. The main rivers in today's state of Punjab are Satluj, Beas and Ravi. These rivers are fed by the waters from melting of snow in Himalayas, so they flow throughout the year i.e. these are perennial rivers.

The state is divided into three geographical regions - Majha, Malwa and Doaba. This is mainly due to separation of these areas by Satluj and Beas rivers. The area between Beas and Ravi is known as Majha and is also called as Bari Doab. The area between Satluj and Beas rivers is called as Doaba and also known as Bist Doab. The area on the south of Satluj River is known as Malwa.

Shivalik hills which are situated at the foothills of Himalayas form the eastern boundary of the state along the state of Himachal Pradesh. The semi-hilly area in this part is locally known as 'Kandi' area. Most of the land of Punjab is fertile plain but one can find the south-east region being semi-arid and desert landscapes on the Thar, or Great Indian, Desert. A belt of swelling hills extends along the northeast at the foot of the Himalayas. Punjab state is situated between the great systems of the Indus and Ganges rivers.

Punjab is classified as Subtropical Semi-arid climate type. Most parts of the state receive abundant rainfall during the monsoon season. The average annual rainfall in the state is around 500mm. In summers, the temperature during the day remains close to 40-45 degree Celsius. The peak summer season is during the period from mid-May to mid-July. The winters are also harsh in the state. During the peak winter season from mid- December to mid-February, the temperature goes down to around 5 degree Celsius.

BRIEF HISTORY:

The Punjab region of India and Pakistan has a historical and cultural link to Indo-Aryan peoples as well as partially to various indigenous communities. As a result of several invasions from Central Asia and the Middle East, many ethnic groups and religions make up the cultural heritage of the Punjab.

The region was originally called Sapta Sindhu, the Vedic land of the seven rivers flowing into the ocean. The Sanskrit name for the region, as mentioned in the Ramayana and Mahabharata for example, was Panchanada which means "Land of the Five Rivers", and was translated to Persian as Punjab after the Muslim conquests. The later name of the region, Punjab, is a compound of two Persian words, Panj (five) and āb (water), introduced to the region by the Turko-Persian conquerors of India, and more formally popularized during the Mughal Empire. Punjab thus means "The Land of Five Waters", referring to the rivers Jhelum, Chenab, Ravi, Sutlej, and Beas. All are tributaries of the Indus River, the Chenab being the largest.

> *"Punjabi culture is one of self-dependence, self-reliance and hard work, which have made Punjabis statistically on average the wealthiest in India. These character traits comes from Punjab's difficult history, particularly due to the number of outside invasions (Aryan, Greeks, Indo-Greeks, Indo-Scythians, Kushans, Indo-Sassanians, Turks, Mughals and Afghans), and retaliation from Punjabis in response to these acts. This heroism of Punjabis was highlighted with Alexander's invasion of Punjab. One of the most notable is the Punjabi King Porus & his army's defense of Punjab. In a letter to his mother, Alexander wrote, "I am involved in the land of a leonine and brave people, where every foot of the ground is like a well of steel, confronting my soldier. You have brought only one son into the world, but everyone in this land can be called an Alexander."*

Some of India's best intellectuals, business people, sports people, artists, military and political leaders come from this state. Punjabis customarily value and show great respect for their traditions and history. Traditional historic Punjabi culture is renowned for its tolerance, progressive and logical approach to life. The state is the location of one of the world's first and oldest civilizations, the Indus Valley Civilization, India's first civilization. As a consequence it has some of the richest cultural history in the world. Their culture was based on their religious beliefs, which could be described as identical to that of Hindus living across North

India today.

The second strongest emergent cultural identity was Jat and Gujjar culture, based on pastoralist, agriculture and ancestor worship, in modern Punjab. Most of the Western regions are descended from Gujjars, whereas the Eastern region is ethnically Jat. Over centuries, Islamic traditions were incorporated into the lives of Punjabi Muslims. These people would often live together marrying others like them and the customs practiced centuries ago are still visible in the way all the castes and religious groups live.

The Indian state of Punjab was created in 1947, when the Partition of India split the former Raj province of Punjab between India and Pakistan. The mostly Muslim western part of the province became Pakistan's Punjab Province; the mostly Sikh and Hindu eastern part became India's Punjab state. Many Hindus and Sikhs lived in the west, and many Muslims lived in the east, and so the partition saw many people displaced and much inter communal violence. Several small Punjabi princely states, including Patiala, also became part of India. In 1950, two separate states were created; Punjab included of the former Raj province of Punjab, while the princely states were combined into a new state, the Patiala and East Punjab States Union (PEPSU). PEPSU consisted of the princely states of Patiala, Nabha, Jind, Kapurthala, Malerkotla, Faridkot and Kalsia. Himachal Pradesh was created as a union territory from several princely states and Kangra District. In 1956, PEPSU was merged into Punjab state, and several northern districts of Punjab in the Himalayas were added to Himachal Pradesh.

On November 1, 1966, most of its predominantly Hindi-speaking areas were separated to form the new state of Haryana. Chandigarh was on the border between the two states, and became a separate union territory which serves as the capital of both Punjab and Haryana.

CULTURE AND TRADITIONS:

The people of Punjab with diversity in nature are the descendants of the Aryan tribes who came to India from the northwest as well as the pre-Aryan population, probably Dravidians who had a highly developed civilization. The surviving of this civilization is found at Rupnagar in the state of Punjab. The social structure of Punjabi which is noted for its diversity in culture is been built by the various groups or the jatis like the invaders which include Greeks, Parthians, Kushans, and Hephthalites.

The Islam force which invaded the state forced several communities like the Jat peasant caste and the Rajput class of landowners to follow the religion and faith of Islam which was more of a deliberate conversion under the influence of the Sufi saints. However the majority of the population of Punjab is the Sikhs which had its origin from the teachings of Nanak, the first Sikh Guru.

Though today there is a small amount of Muslims, Christians and Jain population in the state, Hindus make up the largest minority. The most common language spoken by the people is Punjabi which is also the official language of the state. Apart from the Punjabi's the other ethnic groups belonging to this area is the Shahmukhi, Gurmukhi, Devnagri originating from the region between Pakistan and India. The Punjabi's residing in the East and the West are known as Biradari and these subgroups include Jats, Rajputs, Khatris, Dalits, Gujjar, Syed, Brahmins and many more.

The culture of the people of Punjab is supposed to be one of the old and rich cultures of the world which has a very great history and complexity. The culture of the Punjabi's is widely spread throughout the country for the Punjabi's have settled across the globe. The culture of the Punjabi's shows its diversity and rich cultural heritage which is known for their uniqueness that includes different fields like Philosophy, poetry, spirituality, education, artistry, music, cuisine, science, technology, military warfare, architecture, traditions, values and history. They are very particular about their traditions and relations.

There is a clannishness and high spirits which is exhibited in the lifestyle of the Punjabi people. Every festival or ceremony has predefined rituals which are strictly followed. May it be birth or wedding, hair cutting or a funeral, the adherence to rituals is a must which according to them strengthens a relation and displays a proper social cordiality. People, Culture, Festivals of Punjab collectively form a vivacious base of enlightening social verve. While the people of Punjab are known for their strong determination, the culture of the state presents a multi-hued heritage of ancient civilizations.

The People of Punjab are friendly, hospitable, and hardworking and relish living. This is due to the fact that it usually bore the onslaught of attackers a number of times. People like to live in their present time by enjoying life. Punjabi songs are full of melody. The beats of drum (dhol) and the rhythm of the steel spoon on the dholak is a simple style but add to the exuberance of Punjabi music. The dance styles of Punjab have more flavors with its bhangra, giddha, kikli and sammi. Folk music is the soul of Punjabi culture. Folk music comprises of simple musical instruments like dholak and dhol drum. Punjabi music relates to the zestful people of Punjab. The traditional attire of people is Kurta-pyjama with turban for men. Women prefer Patiala suits as part of their traditional attire. However, the younger generation prefers trendy attire as per the fashion scenario.

CLIMATE:

Punjab is a state with a balanced incorporation of heat in summer, rain in monsoon and cold in winter. The three seasons are so distinctly distributed that you can enjoy each of them individually. Every season has its intrinsic worth. Owing to its north-east location, Punjab experiences both summer and winter to its extreme. It even receives abundant rainfall, which makes the state a very fertile land. The summer season starts from March till July and the maximum temperature rises to 48 degree Celsius. Rainy season from July to September experiences adequate amount of rainfall for the ecosystem. Winter starts from October and continues till February. During this time the state experiences chilling cold conditions and at some places the mercury dips to 10 degree Celsius.

AGRICULTURE AND STAPLE FOOD:

Punjab is one of the most fertile regions on earth. Some two-fifths of Punjab's population is engaged in the agricultural sector, which accounts for a significant segment of the state's gross product. Much of the state's agricultural progress and productivity is attributable to the so-called **Green Revolution**, an international movement launched in the 1960s that introduced not only new agricultural technologies but also high-yielding varieties of wheat and rice.

The region is ideal for growing wheat crop. Rice, sugar cane, fruits and vegetables are also grown. Indian Punjab is called the "Granary of India" or "India's bread-basket." Even bajra is predominantly used in some parts of the state.

Punjab is the largest grown crop is wheat. Other important crops are rice, cotton, sugarcane, pearl millet, maize, barley and fruits. The principal crops of Punjab are barley, wheat, rice, maize and sugarcane. Among the fodder crops are bajra and jowar. In the category of fruits, it produces abundant stock of kinnow (a kind of orange). The main sources of irrigation are canals and tube wells. The Rabi or the spring harvest consists of wheat, gram, barley, potatoes and winter vegetables. The Kharif or the autumn harvest consists of rice, maize, sugarcane, cotton and pulses. The land is highly fertile and so there are plenty of grazing grounds for the cattle and so the people of this region are mostly farmers as well as cattle rearers.

CHARACTERISTICS AND SALIENT FEATURES OF THE CUISINE:

Punjabis are a hardworking and fun loving community which can be experienced in every part of their daily routine. The earliest references to region's food are found in the Vedas, which document the lives of the Aryans in the Punjab. Amazingly the elements mentioned over 6,000 years ago are still extant in this cuisine. This includes dairy-dughd (milk), ghrit (ghee) and dadhi (curd), shak (leafy green vegetables) and a variety of grain. Even today, the staple in the Punjab is grains and vegetables in their basic form.

Ayurvedic texts refer to Vatika - a dumpling of sundried, spice specked delicacy made with lentil paste called vadi .The art of making vadi reached its acme in Amritsar with the arrival of the merchants of Marwar, who were invited by Ram Das, the fourth Guru if the Sikhs, to stream line the trade in the sacred city. There is also reference to vataka or vadha made of soaked coarsely ground and fermented mash (husked urad) daal.

The unhusked mash is the mother of all lentils. Rajmah derives from the word raj mash or the regal mash. Other pulses mentioned are chanak or chaak (channa dal) and alisandaga (identified as kabuli or large channa) that is stated to have reached India with Alexander the Great's troops who came to India via Afghanistan. Punjabis are big-time food lovers, preferring a wide variety in their menu. They are full of life and their food too reflects this liveliness. The people in this state generally go for spicy foods and use mustard oil and ghee to a considerably higher extent.

Punjab's other grand contribution is the dhaba - the roadside eatery that has become a prominent feature on the national and state highways. Earlier frequented only by truck drivers, today it is in vogue to eat at a dhaba- urban or roadside.

<u>Features of the cuisine:</u>

- Punjab being near the border of Pakistan experiences Punjabi-Sikh, Hindu and Muslim diverse culinary influences and the proximity with Persia, Afghanistan and Central Asia gave them a taste for fresh and dried fruits and exotic nuts.
- Punjabi cuisine has always been strongly influenced by Mughal invaders who brought with them the tradition

of the great Tandoor and now Punjabi tandoori cooking is celebrated as one of the most popular cuisine throughout the world.

- One of the salient features Punjabi food is the diverse range of dishes that can suit any palate. The food could range from spicy to sour, and sweet to tangy.
- The natural diet is mostly vegetarian-based rather than meat-based, but still people are consuming chicken, fish and lamb dishes. Sikhism is the most widely followed religion in Punjab, which forbids the consumption of beef (as the cow is a sacred animal) and strongly discourages the consumption of meat.
- Bhunao or roasting is one of the main techniques of Punjabi cuisine specially for non-vegetarian cooking. It brings to mind images of appetizing food.
- Punjab being a land of abundant milk, its related products is an essential part of their everyday or routine cooking. Malai (cream), Curd and buttermilk is a must in every Punjabi meal apart from paneer (cottage cheese), a must in the vegetarian Punjabi menu. Several delectable items are made out of this rather bland derivative of milk. Creations like the Kadai Paneer and Makhani Paneer are basically Punjabi but are well loved all over the country.
- Punjabi's prefer more of wheat products and only on special occasions they prefer rice. Rice is never eaten plain for its always seasoned and flavored with cumin and fried onions and accompanied with Rajma or kadhi.
- Though they don't eat too much of sauces or marinades but prefer some spices adding lot of ghee to their food.
- Most Punjabi menus are made according to the season. The universal favourite is chhole-bathure which is a round-the-year item and is available at every wayside

dhaba anywhere in Northern India.

- In winter, rice is cooked with jaggery - gurwala chawal or with green peas – matarwale chawal or as a delicacy called Rao ki kheer, which is rice cooked on a slow fire for hours together with sugar cane juice.
- During winters the locals sarson-ka-saag (mustard leaves) served with blobs of white butter accompanied by makke-di-roti and tall glass of lassi (churned yogurt- either spiced or sweet or both).
- They also prefer refreshing drinks like kanjee (fermented carrot and mustard paste drink, served in earthen ware —matka) and shikanji (chilled drink made of chili water, lemon juice, salt, sugar black salt powder and black pepper powder).
- Punjabs own signature dishes include matar paneer, dal makhani, Mah ki Dal, Sarson Da Saag Makki Di Roti,Tandoori chicken, Bhuna gosht, Achari Gosht, Amritsari fish,tandoori jheega, paranthas, bhature , tandoori roti and lassi and Dahi Raita that are popular all over India.
- Morning of every Punjabi starts with stuffed paratha with curd and pickle, lunch accompanies Sarson Ka Saag and Makki Ki Roti with mint and onion chutney and dinner usually Mah Ki Dal, Bhunna Gosht, Naan, Tandoori Roti and Dahi Raita.
- All lentils, especially black gram and yellow gram, are a part of Punjabi cuisine. Rajma or Chana are also very popularly used.
- The main masala in a Punjabi dish consists of onion, garlic and ginger and a lot of tomatoes fried in pure ghee.

- Various masalas used in Punjabi cuisines are garam masala -made of cumin seeds, black cardamom seeds, black pepper corn, green cardamom, cinnamon, mace, shahi jeera, bay leaves and dry rose petals, coriander seeds, fennel seeds, cloves and ginger powder, nutmeg. Aromatic garam masala (made of green cardamom, cumin seeds, black pepper corn, cinnamon, cloves and nutmeg). Chaat masala- made of cumin seeds, black pepper corn, black salt, dry pudina (mint), hing (asafetida), tartaric acid, amchoor (mango powder), ajwain (caraway seeds), sonth (ginger powder) and yellow chili powder. Tandoori chaat masala -made of cumin seeds, black pepper corn , black salt, dry pudina, kasoori methi, green cardamom, cloves, cinnamon, ajwain, hing, tartaric acid, mace, mango powder, ginger powder, yellow chili powder, anardana (pomegranate seeds).
- Traditional Indian spices grounded in Ghotna, a conventional kitchen device to grind and crush spices and other ingredients, are generally used in preparing the dishes.
- Though chicken is a favorite with non-vegetarians, fish is also considered a delicacy, especially in the Amritsar region-Amritsari machchhi.
- Food is usually garnished with finely cut coriander leaves and juliennes of ginger.
- Traditional Punjabi thali consists of varied kinds of breads; some are baked in the tandoor such as tandoori roti, laccha paratha, naan and kulcha, while others are dry baked on the tava (pan) like chapatti and jowar ki roti and rumali roti. There are breads that are shallow fried such as parantha and deep-fried such as puri and bhatoora.

- Phirni, a sweet dish made of milk, rice flour and sugar and chilled in earthenware bowls is a typical Punjabi dessert. Punjabi sweet dishes like gulab jamuns and burfi have a strong percentage of khoya again made from milk.

Different Cooking Styles:

Various traditional cooking styles are applied with the villagers still using some of the conventional cooking infrastructures like the Punjabi bhatthi which is similar to a masonry oven. The Punjabi bhatthi is constructed with bricks or mud and clay and covered with a metal at the top. One side of the oven has an opening where wood; grass and bamboo leaves are put to burn the fire. The smoke of such fire emits through a cylinder. The traditional stoves and ovens in Punjab are called Chulla and Bharolli respectively and it is common to find ovens called band chulla and wadda chulla in Punjabi households. Another method of cooking using a traditional heating appliance in the form of a wood-burning stove that comprise of a closed solid metal fire chamber, an adjustable air control and a fire base made of brick is gradually dying out. A variant of such cooking style that has been strongly influenced by Mughal invaders who brought with them become quite popular is the tandoori style that includes preparing various dishes in a clay oven called tandoor. In rural Punjab, the community tandoor or Sanjha Chullah or Kath tandoor are dug in the ground is a meeting place, just like the village well for all the women folk, who bring the kneaded atta (dough) and sometimes marinated meats to have them cooked.

EQUIPMENTS AND UTENSILS USED:

- *Madhani*: It is a wooden churner fixed to a brass pot. It is used for churning out butter from cream.
- *Chakla belan*: Chakla is a small marble or wooden platform and belan is the rolling pin. These are usually made up of wood. They are used for rolling the dough to make various Indian breads such as chapattis and puris.
- Chajj : is a kind of winnowing instrument
- *Kadhai*: it is a deep, concave utensil made up of brass, iron or aluminium and is used for deep fat frying and also general cooking.
- *Kadoo kas* (grater): This equipment has sharp grooves of different sizes meant for grating.
- *Channani* (sieve): It is used to sieve or sift flour and commodities of similar nature. The channani can have removable inserts that have varied sizes of holes for coarse or fine sieving.
- *Masala dani*: It literally translates to _spice box'. It contains the commonly used dry spices, both whole and powdered.
- *Pauni*: A perforated spoon used for frying food commodities.
- *Karchi* (ladle): It is actually a big round spoon for stirring dal or mixing food or even serving it.
- *Tawa*: This flat base equipment is usually made of cast iron is used for making Indian breads such as roti and parathas. They are available in various sizes, depending upon the uses.
- *Loh*: is a large pan used for cooking breads.
- *Patila*: It is generally made up of brass and comes with a lid. It is used when something has to be sautéed, boiled or simmered. It is also used for making gravies and cooking in bulk. These are also available in various sizes.

- *Dechka*: is a brass cooking vessel.
- *Tandoor*: It is a clay oven chamber, which is lit with live charcoal. It is used for baking various Indian breads, kebabs (boti, white meat, fish, prawn etc) and other items.
- *Bhatti*: It is used for grilling kebabs. It is an open fire grill, where coal is the only medium of fire.
- *Khoncha*: It is a flat metal spoon used for stir frying or sautéing the ingredients.
- *Chimta*: These are meant for holding the hot objects e.g. the roti on the open fire or the griddle, turning items in hot oil while deep fat frying.
- *Chaati* : is a large earthen vessel.
- *Ghotna/ danda*: wooden pestles.
- *Hamam dista* (mortar and pestle): It is a pair of tools used to crush, grind, and mix solid substances or masalas. It is usually made of iron but can also be made of marble stone, wood, bamboo, iron, steel, brass and basalt.
- *Ukhli/Dauri/Kundi* : is a mortar used for grinding masalas.
- *Dori danda*: It is a stoneware pot with a log of wood, used for pounding chutneys aor dry spices. The pestle could be either of wood or stone.
- *Takri*: is a scale

SPECIALTIES DURING FESTIVALS AND OTHER OCCASIONS:

- Rajma: These are red kidney beans cooked with ginger, garlic, and tomatoes and flavored with turmeric powder and red chili powder. They are normally paired with the jeera pulow and commonly eaten with desi ghee poured on top.

- Sarson Ki Daag: Fresh mustard leaves are combined with amaranth leaves and braised along with ginger, garlic, onions and tomatoes until they become creamy. This dish is garnished with white butter and eaten with makki ki roti.

- Punj Ratani Dal: It is prepared by cooking five dals with onion and tomatoes, symbolic to the five rivers of Punjab. The most commonly used lentils are chana, split urad, green moong, kidney beans and masoor dal.

- Maa Ki Dal: Broken black lentils are combined with Bengal gram and simmered with onions and tomatoes on a low flame, until it is creamy. It is relished with the wholewheat chapattis.

- Dal Makhani: Black lentils are simmered overnight with tomatoes (finely chopped or puree) and butter on slow simmering charcoals. It is finished with cream and kasoori methi and served with a dollop of butter.

- Amritsari Kulcha: Wholewheat doughis stuffed with fillings ranging from paneer to cauliflower, potatoes, or a mixture of all of the above. It is cooked in the tandoor and served with dollops of butter.

- Pindi Choley/Chana: This dish comes from Rawalpindi, where the chickpeas are boiled with black tea to give it its traditional black colour. These cooked chick peas are then cooked with onions, tomatoes and spices. These are commonly served with bhatura for breakfast or even as snacks.

- Baigan Da Bharta: Large egg plants are char grilled in tandoor until soft and are then peeled. This soft flesh is mixed with little tomato and onion gravy flavoured with spices and chopped coriander leaves.

- Bharwan Shimla Mirch: Tandoori stuffed shimla mirch.
- Tandoori Jheenga: Tandoori prawn enriched with tandoori masala.
- Tandoori Chicken: Whole chicken is de – skinned and marinated overnight with curd, red chilli powder and spices. Normally the bird weighs around 800gm to 900gm after dressing. It is then skewered and cooked in the tandoor. Its reddish colour with typical flavour of the charcoal roast makes it a gourmet's delight.
- Maah Chhole Di Daal: It is a dal preparation made of urad dal, rajma, channa dal, enriched with cream and desi ghee.
- Amritsari Kulcha: Potato cauliflower, paneer stuffed roti cooked in tandoor.
- Murgh Butter Masala: Tandoor cooked chicken is cooked in creamy tomato gravy (in base of butter) along with ginger garlic paste, red chilli powder and flavoured with kasoori methi. The gravy of tomatoes is also known as makhni gravy. This gravy adds moisture to the tandoori chicken which is otherwise eaten dry.
- Rara Gosht: A rich heavy and thick mutton preparation in which mutton boti and mutton mince is cooked together with onion and masalas till done.
- Murgh Makhni: Tandoori chicken in tomato based rich gravy which is enriched by
- addition of cashew nut cream and butter.
- Fish Amritsari: The cubes of fish are first marinated in salt, red chilli powdet and lemon juice. A thick batter is prepared with besan, ajwain, red chilli powder and salt.
- The fish is coated in this batter and the deep fat fried. It is served with aamchoor powder sprinkled on top and with lemon wedges.

- Multani Tikka: Crispy ajwain flavored paneer and onion tikka, served with tandoor kebab masala.
- Phirnee: It is a traditional dessert served normally during the summer months. Soaked rice is ground into a paste and then added to boiling sweet milk. This is cooked until thickened and poured into terracotta pots. The extra moisture from the pudding is soaked by the earthenware pot and thus the pudding sets soft yet firm. It is then garnished with slivers of pistachio and strands of saffron.

FESTIVITIES:

Lohri: In Punjab, wheat is the main winter crop, which is sown in October and harvested in March or April. In January, the fields come up with the promise of a golden harvest, and farmers celebrate Lohri during this rest period before the cutting and gathering of crops. For Punjabis, this is more than just a festival; it is also an example of a way of life. Lohri is a festival of zeal and verve and marks the culmination of the chilly winter. In true spirit of the Punjabi culture, men and women perform Bhangra and Giddha, popular Punjabi folk dances, around a bonfire. Enthusiastic children go from house to house singing songs and people oblige them generously by giving them money and eatables as offering for the festival. Logs of wood are piled together for a bonfire, and friends and relatives gather around it. They go around the fire three times, giving offerings of popcorns, peanuts, rayveri and sweets. Then, to the beat of the dhol (traditional Indian drum), people dance around the fire. Prasad of til, peanuts, rayveri, puffed rice, popcorn, gajak and sweets are distributed. This symbolizes a prayer to Agni for abundant crops and prosperity. Lohri is also an auspicious occasion to celebrate a newly born baby's or a new bride's arrival in the family. The day ends with a traditional feast of sarson da saag and makki di roti and a dessert of Rau di kheer (a dessert made of sugarcane juice and rice). The purpose of the Lohri harvest ceremony is to thank the God for his care and protection. During this festival the people prepare large quantities of food and drink, and make merry throughout the day and night. Therefore everyone looked forward to this day.

Maghi: The very next day of the Lohri is marked as the Makar sankranti or the Maghi celebration in the form of local fairs and melas. While the female folk are engrossed in cooking the dish of the day, kheer, a lot of donations and charities take place and the day is passed with singsongs and dances.

Baisakhi: Baisakhi, celebrated with joyous music and dancing, is New Year's Day in Punjab. It falls on April 13, though once in 36 years it occurs on 14th April. It was on this day that the tenth Sikh Guru, Guru Gobind Singh, founded the Khalsa (the Sikh brotherhood) in 1699. The Sikhs, therefore, celebrate this festival as a collective birthday. A sweet dish called Anaarse is prepared made using fermented batter (rice or wheat) and shaped into a pebble-shape.

Basant Panchami: It is a festival that marks the onset of spring. It is a brightly colored festival, with yellow as a symbolic color of harvest. This festival has a range of Punjabi foods like the main course ones such as biryani, but the lighter and excitable ones like jalaibees and pakoras are also common. A number of sweet drinks are quite common as well at this time of the year. These are refreshing and symbolize the joy during the season. Aside from the festivals like Basant Panchami, Punjabi food traditions include the all-important heavy main courses at weddings. These might include heavy rice dishes and curries as well. These are accompanied with salads and other side dishes as well.

Guru Purab: The Sikh festivals are celebrated as Guru purabs. They either mark the birth anniversary or the martyrdom of any Sikh guru. The devotees attend langar or the common meals where everyone eats the same food irrespective of caste, class, or creed. Devotees offer their services for cooking food, cleaning the Gurdwara or carrying out other chores. This is called the Kar Seva. The food is served with the spirit of seva (service) and bhakti (devotion). On Guru Arjan Dev's martyrdom day, sweetened milk is offered to passers-by.

Holla Mohalla: Holla Mohalla is a Sikh festival celebrated in the month of Phalguna , a day after Holi. An annual festival held at Anandpur Sahib in Punjab, Hola Mohalla was started by the tenth Sikh Guru, Gobind Singh, as a gathering of Sikhs for military exercises and mock battles on the day following the festival of Holi. It reminds the people of valor and defense preparedness, concepts dear to the Tenth Guru who was at that time battling the Mughal Empire. On this three-day festival mock battles are held followed by music and poetry competitions. The Nihang Sikhs (members of the Sikh army that was founded by Guru Govind Singh) in their carry on the martial tradition with mock battles and displays of swordsmanship and horse riding. They perform daring feats, such as Gatka (mock encounters), tent pegging, bareback horse-riding and standing erect on two speeding horses. The festival culminates with a procession, wherein the —panj pyaaras are adorned with traditional attires in blue and saffron colour.

Teeyan: A lively and refreshing dance festival, mostly for women, Teeyan is celebrated in the blooming season of spring. The upbeat nature feeds the rhythm in these women. The traditional folk dance of Punjab, —Gidda‖ is performed in full force during this festival, which is a magnificent sight to behold. The energizing dance is bound to leave you blown away for days.

Tikka: Also, known as —Bhai Dooj‖, Tikka is a festival celebrating the bond of brothers and sisters. Herein, the sister puts a red symbol on the forehead of the brother, called tikka which is meant for the long life of his brother. The brother is turn gives gifts as a token of his love and affection towards his sister. Everyone dresses up in new clothes and feels a loving sense of siblinghood in them.

Chappar Mela: A numerically small, but symbolically huge fair is held in the Chappar district of Ludhiana. The festival celebrates the supposed Lord of snakes, who is believed to pacify the venom of snakes and also bless families with children, if they are seeking them. The fair is a cultural phenomenon where thousands of believers participate annually.

Jor Mela: Commemorating the martyred sons of Guru Gobind Singh, the Jor Mela is held in Fatehgarh Sahib. The festival is a highly revered one, which is attended by many religious followers, who are moved by a feeling of belongingness to their community. The festival is marked by a recital of the holy book of Sikhs, followed by a procession on the streets.

Hariballabh Sangeet Mela: Remembering an important saint-musician, Swami Haribhallabh, this fair is held annually near his 70 amadhi. The music maestro is remembered through a gallant display of soothing musical notes and divine voices. Many classical musicians attend the festival and offer their voices to the celebration of the great saint.

Kila Raipur Sports Festival: Kila Raipur Sports Festival, popularly known as the Rural Olympics, is held annually in Kila Raipur (near Ludhiana), in Punjab, India. This festival which is popularly known as rural Olympics of Punjab . This rural sports festival takes place over 3 days in January/ February and over 4000 men and women participate in it. Activities during the fest include bullock cart race, rope pulling, Tirinjen, Kikli, Gheeta Pathar, Khidu, Kokla Chhapaki, Chicho Chich Ganerian, Lukan Miti, Kidi Kada or Stapoo, Ghaggar Phissi, Kabbadi, Rasa Kashi, Akharas among others

Rose Festival: Rose Festival is one of the prime events in Chandigarh. Chandigarh is a centre of commerce or various Botanical products and the Rose Garden is specially the most reputed for the exquisite varieties of Roses that are on exhibition. 30 acres of land is allotted for the Rose Garden and every year festivals are held at this place for the exhibition of the Roses that bloom in the garden of Chandigarh.

COMMUNITY FOODS:

Punjabi eating style: Winter, in Punjab, brings in the season of the famous makki ki roti (maize flour bread) and sarson ka saag (mustard leaf gravy). No meal is complete without a serving of lassi (sweet or salted drink made with curd) or fresh curd and white butter which is consumed in large quantities. Connoisseurs of the cuisine say that the gravy component of Punjabi cuisine came from the Mughals. The most popular example is the murg makhani. It served the state well to combine this influence in its cooking since it had a lot of pure ghee and butter. Murg makhani also provided a balance to tandoori chicken, which was dry because it was charcoal cooked. Nans and parathas, rotis made of maize flour are typical Punjabi breads. Of course, over the years the roti has been modified to add more variety, so there is the rumali roti, the naan and the laccha parathas, all cooked in the tandoor.

Langar: The institution of the Sikh Langar or free kitchen was started by the first Sikh Guru, Guru Nanak. It was designed to uphold the principle of equality between all people regardless of religion, caste, colour, creed, age, gender or social status, a revolutionary concept in the caste-ordered society of 16th century India where Sikhism began. In addition to the ideals of equality, the tradition of Langar expresses the ethics of sharing, community, inclusiveness and oneness of all humankind.

Origin of word 'Langar': Guru ka Langar (lit. 'Gurus' communal dining-hall) is a community kitchen run in the name of the Guru. Often referred to as the Guru's Kitchen, it is usually a small room attached to a gurdwara, but at larger gurdwaras, such as the Harmandir Sahib, it takes on the look of a military kitchen with tasks arranged so that teams of sewadars prepare tons of food (all meals are vegetarian) for thousands of the Gurus' guests daily. Langar, is said to be a Persian word that translates as 'an almshouse', 'an asylum for the poor and the destitute', 'a public kitchen once kept by a great man for his followers and dependants, holy persons and the needy.' Some scholars trace the word Langar to Sanskrit Analgarh (cooking room). In Persian, the specific term langar has been in use in an identical sense. In addition to the word itself, the institution of langar is also traceable in the Persian tradition. Langars were a common feature of the Sufi centres in the twelfth and thirteenth centuries. Even today some dargahs, or shrines commemorating Sufi saints, run langars, like Khwaja Mu'in ud-Din Chishti's at Ajmer.

<u>Rules concerning the tradition of Langar:</u>

- Simple vegetarian meals
- It is prepared by devotees who recite Gurbani while preparing the langar
- It is served after performing Ardas.
- The food distributed in Pangat without any prejudice or discrimination
- All food must be fresh, clean and hygienically prepared

Amar Das the third guru formalized the institution of langar, the guru's free kitchen, uniting the Sikhs by establishing two key concepts:

Pangat – One family compiled of all of humanity, regardless of caste, color, or creed, sitting together cross legged in lines, forming rows without discrimination or consideration of rank or position.

Sangat – The ennobling influence of people, who aspire to truthful living, and congregate with like-minded company for the purpose of uttering the name of one God in the presence of the Guru Granth.

When preparing food for the Langar, the mouth and nose will be covered by a piece of cloth known as a "parna". Also during the preparation due regard is made to purity, hygiene and cleaniness, the sevadars (selfless workers) will normally utter Gurbani and refrain from speaking if possible.

When the Langar is ready, a small portion of each of the dishes is placed in a plate or bowls and placed in front of the Sri Guru Granth Sahib and a prayer called the Ardas is performed. The Ardas is a petition to God; a prayer to thank the Creators for all His gifts and blessings. A steel kirpan is passed through each item of food, after the "Guru- prashad" has been blessed. When serving the Langar, the servers must observe strict rules of cleanliness and hygiene. Servers should not touch the serving utensils to the plates of those they serve. When serving foods by hand, such as chapatis or fruit, the servers' hands should not touch the hand or plate of those they are serving. Those serving should wait until all others have been completely served before they sit down to eat themselves. It is advisable not to leave any leftovers.

Since some Sikhs believe that it is against the basics of Sikhi to eat meat, fish or eggs, hence non-vegetarian foods of this sort is neither served nor brought onto the Gurdwara premises. Others believe that the reason vegetarian food is served in Gurdwaras is so that people of all backgrounds can consume the food without any anxiety about their particular dietary requirement and to promote complete equality among all the peoples of the world. Alcoholic and narcotic substances are stringently against the Sikh diet, hence these with any meat products are strictly not allowed on Gurdwara premises.

Punjab's other grand contribution is the dhaba - the roadside eatery that has become a prominent feature on the national and state highways. Earlier frequented only by truck drivers, today it is in vogue to eat at a dhaba-urban or roadside.

RECIPES FROM THE PUNJABI CUISINE:

<u>*Fish Amritsari*</u>

Ingredients

- King Fish cut into fingers 600 grams
- Gram Flour 1 cup
- Red chilli powder 1 tablespoon
- Salt to taste
- Carom seeds (ajwain) 1 teaspoon
- Ginger paste 2 tablespoons
- Garlic paste 2 tablespoons
- Lemon juice 1 tablespoon
- Oil to deep fry
- Egg 1
- Chaat masala 1 teaspoon
- Lemons cut into wedges 2

Method

- Take the fish fingers in a bowl. Add red chilli powder, salt, carom seeds, ginger paste, garlic paste, lemon juice, gram flour and mix well. Set aside. Heat sufficient oil in a kadai.
- Break an egg into the fish mixture and mix. Put the fingers, a few at a time, into the hot oil and deep fry till almost done.
- Drain and place on an absorbent paper. Deep fry again just before serving till golden and crisp.

- Drain and place on an absorbent paper. Serve hot, sprinkled with chaat masala and lemon wedges.

Murgh Patiala

Ingredients

- Chicken (Bone cut) into 4 pieces on the bone 800 grams
- Yogurt 2 tablespoons
- Cumin seeds 1 ½ teaspoons
- Cinnamon 1 inch
- Cloves 4-5
- Green cardamoms 4-5
- Black cardamoms 2-3
- Black peppercorns 1 tablespoon
- Salt to taste
- Red chilli powder 2 teaspoons
- Yogurt ¼cup
- Garlic paste 1 tablespoon
- Ginger paste 1 tablespoon
- Oil 4 tablespoons
- Onions grated 4-5 medium
- Dried red chillies 2-3
- Tomato puree 3-4 teaspoons
- Turmeric powder ½ teaspoon
- Green chillies 3-4

Method

- Dry roast coriander seeds, cumin seeds, cinnamon, cloves, green cardamoms, black cardamoms and black peppercorns till fragrant. Set aside to cool.

- Place the chicken in a bowl, add salt, red chilli powder and yogurt and mix well.
- Add garlic paste and ginger paste and mix again and keep in the refrigerator to marinate for 15-20 minutes.
- Heat oil in a non-stick pan. Add onions and sauté till well browned.
- Coarsely grind the roasted spices with dried red chillies.
- Add tomato puree, turmeric powder and broken green chillies to the onions in the pan.
- Mix well and sauté for 3-4 minutes. Add the marinated chicken and mix well.
- Add ½ the spice powder and mix well. Add 2-3 tbsps water and mix again.
- Cover and cook till the chicken is done.
- Add the remaining spice powder and mix well, cover and cook on low heat for 10 minutes.
- Remove from heat and let it stand for a few minutes before serving.
- Serve hot.

Matar Methi Malai

Ingredients
   For masala paste:

- 2 tsp oil
- 1 onion, slice
- 2 chilli, slit
- 1 tsp ginger garlic paste
- ¼ cup cashew / kaju, soaked

For curry:

- 3 tsp oil
- 1 tsp cumin / jeera
- 2 cup fenugreek / methi, finely chopped
- 1 cup water
- ½ cup cream
- 1 cup peas / matar
- ½ tsp sugar
- ¾ tsp salt
- ¼ tsp garam masala

Method

- In a large kadai heat 3 tsp oil and splutter 1 tsp cumin.
- Further, add the prepared masala paste and saute well.
- Saute until the oil is separated from sides.
- Add in 2 cup fenugreek and saute for 2 minutes.
- Add in 1 cup water and ½ cup cream.
- Mix well making sure the cream is well combined.
- Add in 1 cup peas, ½ tsp sugar and ¾ tsp salt.
- Mix well, cover and boil for 8-10 minutes or until the peas are cooked well.
- The curry turns creamy, adjust the consistency as required.
- Now add ¼ tsp garam masala and mix well.
- Finally, enjoy methi matar malai with roti or paratha.

Sarson Da Saag

Ingredients

- Fresh mustard leaves (sarson) 5 bunches
- Fresh spinach leaves (palak) 1 bunch

- Bathua 1 bunch
- Olive oil 5 tablespoons
- Ginger sliced 2 one-inch pieces
- Garlic sliced 6-8 cloves
- Onions sliced 2 medium
- Green chillies 4
- Salt to taste
- Cornmeal 2 tablespoons

Method

- Heat three tablespoons olive oil in a pan, add ginger, garlic and onion and sauté for two to three minutes. Roughly chop mustard leaves.
- Add to pan and stir. Roughly chop spinach and bathua. Add to pan and stir. Break the green chillies and add to the pan.
- Add salt to taste and stir well. Let it cook till the greens turn soft.
- Add cornmeal dissolved in a little water and continue to cook till the greens are completely cooked. Cool and grind to a coarse paste.
- Transfer into the pan. Add the remaining olive oil and mix. Simmer for two to three minutes. Serve hot with makki ki roti.

Dhabbe Di Daal

Ingredients

- ¼cup drained,soaked split black gram
- ½ cup drained,soaked black beans

- 1 tablespoon chopped garlic
- 3 medium chopped tomato
- ½ tablespoon cumin powder
- 1 tablespoon roasted dried fenugreek leaves
- 3 tablespoon butter
- ¼cup drained,soaked red kidney beans
- 2 medium chopped onion
- 3 sliced and slit green chilli
- 6 tablespoon Refined oil
- 2 teaspoon Red chilli powder
- ¼cup chopped coriander leaves
- 1 teaspoon salt

Method

- To make this special recipe, clean, wash and soak black beans, split bengal gram and red kidney beans in sufficient water for at least 6 hours.
- When all the dals are soaked, drain the extra water. Then in a pressure cooker, add 4 cups of water and cook the drained dals on high heat in a cooker till 4 whistles and then cook on slow fire for around 30 minutes. Keep the cooked dals aside.
- Now take a pan and heat oil in it and add chopped onion, stir fry the onions till they turn golden brown and translucent.
- Add garlic and green chillies in the onions, and stir fry for another 10-15 minutes.
- Now add red chilli powder and cumin powder in the stir-fried onions, and cook for a minute.
- Then add tomatoes and stir fry on high flame for around 3-4 minutes or till the masala leaves oil. Now add salt in it, mix it well, and remove from fire.

- Add this stir-fried masala to the cooked dals in the pressure cooker, and cook for around 5 minutes.
- Top the prepared dal with butter and garnish it with freshly chopped coriander, and transfer the contents in a serving bowl.
- Crush roasted dry fenugreek leaves between the palms, sprinkle on the dal and serve it hot.

Makki Di Roti

Ingredients

- 1 cup maize flour
- 1 pinch red chilli powder
- boiling water as required
- 1 ½ tablespoon ghee
- ½ teaspoon salt
- 1 handful finely chopped fenugreek leaves (methi)
- 1 tablespoon butter

Method

- Start with sifting the maize flour with salt. Once, you have mixed the flour with salt, add the finely chopped fenugreek leaves along with red chilli powder and ghee. Mix all the Ingredients completely.
- Next, add hot water in the maize flour and fenugreek leaves mixture, and knead with soft hands. After making a soft dough, take equal portions of the dough and make medium sized balls. Dust the dough with some flour and

flatten it into a roti.

- Now, put a tawa or a pan over medium flame and let it heat. When the tawa is hot enough, put the roti on it and cook. You don't need to apply ghee, oil or any kind of butter on it, as they are already present in the dough, which is enough to grease it.
- If you think, the roti is too dry, you can pour some drops of melted ghee and cook on both sides. When the roti is cooked, transfer in a serving plate and apply butter on the rotis. Serve hot with sarson ka saag.

Dodhi Halwa

Ingredients

- 2½ cups grated Dudhi (bottle gourd/lauki)
- 1 cup (250 ml) Full Fat Milk
- 3 tablespoons Condensed Milk
- 2 tablespoons Ghee (clarified butter)
- 3 tablespoons Sugar
- 10 Cashew Nuts, chopped
- 10 Almonds, chopped
- 15 Raisins
- ¼teaspoon Cardamom Powder

Method

- To grate the dudhi, first peel it and then wash it in running water. After that, grate it from all sides and discard center part having seeds. Squeeze out water from grated dudhi completely.

- Heat ghee in a pan over medium flame. Add grated dudhi.
- Sauté it for 3-4 minutes, stirring continuously.
- Add milk and condensed milk; mix well and bring mixture to a boil.
- When it starts boiling, reduce flame to low and cook it until almost milk is absorbed. It will take approx. 10-15 minutes. Stir occasionally in between to prevent sticking. Add sugar, chopped cashew nuts, raisins and chopped almonds.

Paneer Amritsari

Ingredients

- 1 cup Paneer (Homemade Cottage Cheese)
- 1 cup Homemade tomato puree
- 1 Onion , finely chopped
- 2 cloves Garlic
- 1 Green Chilli
- 1 inch Ginger
- 5 Cashew nuts
- 2 Cloves (Laung)
- 1 teaspoon Ajwain (Carom seeds)
- 1 teaspoon Garam masala powder
- 1 teaspoon Turmeric powder (Haldi)
- 1-½ teaspoon Coriander Powder (Dhania)
- ½ teaspoon Red chilli powder
- ½ teaspoon Sugar
- Salt
- 1 tablespoon Cooking oil
- Coriander (Dhania) Leaves , chopped for garnish

Method

- To begin making the Amritsari Ajwaini Paneer recipe, we will first make a paste of onion, garlic, ginger and green chillies to a fine paste. Keep this mixture aside.
- Next make a fine paste of the cashew nuts, adding very little water. Keep aside.
- Using a pestle and motor pound ajwain and cloves to a fine powder. Keep aside.
- Heat oil in a heavy bottomed pan on medium heat; add the onion paste and saute for a few minutes; you will notice that the onion mixture begins to absorb all the oil and will look dry. Resist the temptation to add more oil at this point. Continue to saute the onions on medium heat until the raw smell goes away.
- Stir in the turmeric powder, pounded spices and garam masala stir well for a couple of more minutes.
- Add in the pureed tomatoes, coriander powder, red chilli powder, salt. Cover the pan and simmer the ajwaini paneer for 4-5 minutes.
- Stir in the cashewnut paste, sugar and simmer for about a minute. Finally stir in the paneer cubes, garnish with coriander leaves and serve hot with Naans or Tawa Parathas.

Methi Murg

Ingredients

- ¾ Kg chicken (boneless, cut into medium sized pieces)
- 1 medium onions, finely chopped

- 2 medium tomatoes (grind to a smooth paste), finely chopped
- 4-5 tbspcooking oil
- 1 tsp shahi jeera (black cumin seeds)
- 10-12 fresh curry leaves
- to taste salt
- 1 tsp turmeric (pasupu)
- 2 ½ tsp ginger and garlic paste
- 1 ½ tsp cumin powder
- 1 ½ tsp coriander powder
- 3 tsp red chilli powder (adjust according to your taste)
- 1 cup water (add more if required)
- 2 tbspyogurt (whisk it with a fork smoothly and set aside)
- 2 cups fresh methi leaves (fenugreek leaves), finely chopped
- 2 tsp garam masala powder
- 2 tbspcoriander leaves , finely chopped

Method

- In a wide bottomed vessel, heat oil. On low heat, add shahi jeera and fry for a few seconds. Add curry leaves, toss them and then add chopped onions, salt and turmeric.
- Increase the flame to medium and fry till the onions turn golden brown (around 8 minutes).
- Add ginger and garlic paste and fry for 1-2 minutes till the raw smell disappears.
- Add chicken add cumin powder, coriander powder, chilli powder, mix well, cover and cook for 4-5 minutes stirring in between.

- Add tomato paste, water and bring it to boil on high flame.
- When the gravy starts boiling reduce the flame to medium, cover and cook for around 10 - 15 minutes or till the chicken is tender and the gravy starts turning thick. By this time the oil starts floating on top of the gravy.
- Add whisked yoghurt, gently mix, add freshly chopped methi leaves, gently mix so the chicken pieces do not break.
- Lower the flame and allow to cook uncovered for 5 minutes.
- Just before turning off the heat, add garam masala powder, mix well, adjust salt and chilli powder if required.
- Garnish with freshly chopped coriander leaves.
- Serve hot with steamed basmati rice, rotis or naan.

Dal Fry

Ingredients

- ¾ cup Tur (Arhar Dal /Pigeon peas spilt and skinned)
- 2 tablespoons Butter
- 1 tablespoon (Oil)
- 2 cloves Garlic (smashed)
- ½ teaspoon Garlic Paste
- ½ teaspoon Ginger Paste
- 2 Chilies, Green (slit lengthwise)
- 1 Onion (finely chopped)
- 2 Tomatoes (finely chopped)
- ½ teaspoon Chili Powder

- 1 teaspoon Dhaniya (or Coriander Powder)
- ½ teaspoon Jeera (or Cumin Powder)
- ½ teaspoon Turmeric (Powder)
- ½ teaspoon Garam Masala (Powder)
- 1 tablespoon Kasuri Methi
- 1 Lemon
- Salt to taste
- Coriander (Chopped for topping)

Method

- Pressure cook the dal with 2 ½ cups water till completely cooked through and can be mashed easily between two fingers. Use a wire whisk or spoon to mash the dal further so it's almost smooth.
- Heat oil and butter in a pan and smashed garlic. Fry the garlic till light brown, without burning it and add the slit green chilies, ginger and garlic paste.
- Cook for 30 seconds and add onions. Stir fry the onions till they are translucent and add tomatoes, spices and salt.
- Cook till the tomatoes completely break down and become pasty. At this point, stir in the dal along with some water if required. Bring this to a boil and simmer for 5-7 minutes.
- Dry roast the kasuri methi in another pan for a minute or so. Grind it to a powder and mix it in the dal along with juice from the lemon. Switch off the flame and stir in chopped coriander.
- Serve hot with rice, pickle, sliced onions and rotis.

Dahi-Karela

Ingredient

- 4 large bitter gourd
- 1 ½ medium tomato
- ½ teaspoon turmeric
- 1 tablespoon refined oil
- 4 leaves coriander leaves
- 1 ½ medium onion
- ¼cup yoghurt (curd)
- 1 tablespoon coriander powder
- ½ teaspoon garam masala powder
- ½ teaspoon red chilli powder

Method

- To prepare this interesting karela recipe, scrape the karelas. Next, remove the seeds from them by cutting open.
- To remove the bitterness of the karelas, rub salt over them and keep them aside.
- Then take a pan and heat oil to shallow fry the karelas. Drain out the excess oil using a paper towel and set aside. Meanwhile, chop the onions and tomatoes.
- In another pan, start frying the chopped onion and tomatoes. Then add the spices and cook for 2- 3 minutes. Beat the yogurt for a few minutes and then add it to this pan and keep stirring.
- Now add the fried karelas. Cook for around 10 minutes over medium flame. Once done, turn off the gas knob.
- Lastly, transfer it to a serving bowl. Garnish with coriander leaves and serve hot.

Sabz Makhani

Ingredient

- Cauliflower – 100 grams
- Capsicum – 100 grams
- Baby corn – 4
- Carrots – 2
- Tomatoes – 4 (300 grams)
- Green chilly – 1
- Ginger – 1 inch piece
- Green coriander – 3 to 4 tbsp(finely chopped)
- Butter – 2 to 3 tbsp
- Cream – ½ cup (100 grams)
- Oil – 2 to 3 tbsp
- Cumin seeds – 1 tsp
- Brown cardamom – 1
- Black peppercorns – 6 to 7
- Clove – 2
- Cinnamon stick – ½ inch piece
- Coriander powder – 1 tsp
- Red chilly powder – ½ tsp
- Turmeric powder – ½ tsp
- Salt – 1 tsp or to taste

Method

- Cut each tomato into four parts. Peel the ginger and dice it into rough chunks and cut the chilies into two halves.
- Heat a pan with 2 tbspof oil. Now to it add cumin seeds. When the seeds crackle, add chopped tomato-ginger-green chilly, coriander powder, turmeric powder, whole

spices - cinnamon, black pepper and brown cardamom (peeled). Mix everything really well. Cover and cook for 2 minutes until tomatoes get tender.

- Remove seeds from capsicum and cut down into 1-1 inch chunks, chop baby corns as well into ½ - ½ inch chunks and carrots into ½ - ¾ inch chunks as well.

- Check the tomatoes after cutting the veggies. When the tomatoes turn soft, turn off the flame and let the spices cool down a little. Then place these spices in a mixer jar and grind them finely.

- Saute the veggies until they get crunchy. For this, add 2 to 3 tbspbutter and let it melt. Add chopped veggies to the melted butter and mix well. Cover and cook the sabzi for 2 minutes until crunchy. Keep the flame low.

- Prepare gravy on another flame. Add ground masala in the wok and stir constantly to cook. Now add cream to the sabzi and cook until gravy starts simmering. When the gravy starts simmering add ½ cup water into it and let the gravy come to simmer again.

- After 2 minutes, veggies have turned soft, turn off the flame.

- When the gravy starts simmering add salt, red chilli powder and some green coriander to it. Gravy is ready, mix slightly crunchy veggies to it and mix well. Cover and let the sabzi cook for 4 to 5 minutes on low flame.

- Check the sabzi after 5 minute. Sabzi is now ready, transfer it to a serving bowl and garnish with some green coriander. Palatable and super yummy mix veg makhani is ready. Serve this flavorsome and mouth watering sabzi with naan, chapatti, parantha or poori and relish eating.

Missi Roti

Ingredient

- Gram Flour (besan) 2 cups
- Whole Wheat Flour (atta) ¾ cup
- Cumin seeds ½ teaspoon
- Carom seeds (ajwain) ¼teaspoon
- Peppercorns 5-6
- Dried pomegranate seeds (anardana) 1 tablespoon
- Green chillies chopped 3
- Onion chopped 1 medium
- Salt to taste
- Turmeric powder ½ teaspoon
- Fresh coriander leaves chopped 2 tablespoons
- Oil 1 tablespoon + for greasing
- Butter as required

Method

- Take gram flour and whole wheat flour in a bowl. Roast cumin seeds, carom seeds, peppercorns and dry pomegranate seeds. Pound them to a powder.
- Add green chilies, onion, salt, turmeric powder, coriander leaves and mix well. Add sufficient water and knead. Add one tablespoon of oil and the pounded spice powder and knead into dough.
- Cover and rest the dough for about fifteen minutes. Divide into sixteen equal portions and roll into balls. Further roll each portion into a roti.
- Heat a tawa and roast the rotis with a little oil till both sides are well done. Serve hot with a dollop of butter.

Gajar Ka Halwa

Ingredient

- 1 kg or 4 cup grated carrot / gajar
- 4 cup full cream milk
- 1 cup sugar
- 2 tsp ghee
- 8-10 unsalted whole or chopped cashews
- 8-10 unsalted roasted almonds
- 12-15 golden raisins

Method

- Wash, peel and grate the carrots (gajar).
- In a wide open pan add ghee and all the dry fruits. Roast it for one minute.
- Add grated carrot to the same pan. Carrot needs to be cooked only for 2 to 3 minutes until they turn soft as seen in below picture.
- Now add 4 cup of milk. Try to use full cream milk instead of light milk.
- Mix well and let the milk comes to boil. Stir in between so that milk does not get stick to bottom.
- Cook carrot and milk for 30 minutes on low flame. All the milk should be evaporated leaving behind thick khoya.
- Once more than ½ of milk evaporates add 1 cup of sugar. Mix it well with milk.
- Once again, cook the carrots for 30 minutes in a low flame until all the milk evaporates.

- Your Gajar Halwa is ready. Garnish it with dry fruits. Serve it warm or cold depending upon your preferences.

CHAPTER THREE

Delhi – The National Capital Region for a Reason

Delhi is the traditional and present day capital of India. It is the third largest city of the world. It is also the second largest metropolis in India after Mumbai. Delhi is also one of the oldest continually inhabited cities of India. There is no such thing as typical cuisines of Delhi. This is so because there is no specific identity of the city. With time, people from different areas of India came and settled, making Delhi an assortment of delicacies. Slowly and gradually, Delhi assumed some of the aspects of the identity of all the types of people living in it, making multiple identities for itself. This has in turn molded Delhi culture in such a way that the same gets reflected in the behavior and activities of the people. So, it can be conveniently said that the culture of Delhi is an union of different cultures, particularly the culture of the neighboring states like Uttar Pradesh, Haryana, Punjab, and Rajasthan. .

GEOGRAPHY:

Almost entirely within the Gangetic plains, Delhi can be divided into 3 segments - the Yamuna flood plain, the Ridge and the Plain. The Yamuna flood plains are somewhat low-lying and sandy and are subjected to recurrent floods. This area is also called Khadar. The ridge constitutes the most dominating physiographic features of this territory. It originates from the Aravalli hills of Rajasthan and entering the union territory from the south extends in a north eastern direction. It encircles the city on the North West and west.

Delhi stands at 77.12° E longitude and 28.38° N latitude in a triangle formed by the Yamuna river in the east and spurs from the Aravalli range in the west and south, and is spread over 1483 sq.km area. It is surrounded by the state of Haryana on all sides except east where it borders with Uttar Pradesh state. It is traversed by the River Yamuna. Agra Canal, Hindon Canal and the Yamuna Canal supply water to Delhi.

The point near Bhatti has a height of 1045 feet. Tughlqabad fort is located on one of the highest spurs of the ridge. Leaving aside the Yamuna flood plain (khadar) and the ridge, the entire area of the national capital territory of Delhi is categorized as Bangar or the plain. A major proportion of the city is plain and on this are located Delhi, New Delhi and Delhi cantonment along with a vast stretches of numerous villages.

BRIEF HISTORY:

Delhi, the National Capital of India has a strong historical background. It was ruled by some of the most powerful emperors in Indian history. The history of the city is as old as the epic Mahabharata. The town then was known as Indraprastha, where Pandavas used to live. In due course eight more cities came alive adjacent to Indraprastha: Lal Kot, Siri, Dinpanah, Quila Rai Pithora, Ferozabad, Jahanpanah, Tughlakabad and Shahjahanabad.

Delhi has been a witness to the political turmoil for over five centuries. It was ruled by the Mughals in succession to Khiljis and Tughlaqs. In 1192 the legions of the Afghan warrior Muhammad of Ghori captured the Rajput town, and the Delhi Sultanate was established (1206).

The invasion of Delhi by Timur in 1398 put an end to the sultanate; the Lodis, last of the Delhi sultans, gave way to Babur, who, after the battle of Panipat in 1526, founded the Mughal Empire. The early Mughal emperors favoured Agra as their capital, and Delhi became their permanent seat only after Shah Jahan built (1638) the walls of Old Delhi.

From Hindu Kings to Muslim Sultans, the reins of the city kept shifting from one ruler to another. The soils of the city smell of blood, sacrifices and love for the nation. The old 'Havelis' and edifices from the past stand silent but their silence also speaks volumes for their owners and people who lived here centuries back. In the year 1803 AD, the city came under the British rule.

In 1911, British shifted their capital from Calcutta to Delhi. It again became the center of all the governing activities. But, the city has the reputation of over throwing the occupants of its throne. It included the British and the current political parties that have had the honor of leading free India. After independence in 1947, New Delhi was officially declared as the Capital of India.

CLIMATE:

The climatic conditions of Delhi are similar to that of the temperate grasslands with hot, dry summers, and cold winters. That is why, it is said that Delhi climate alone can take tourists to a different climate zone. For example, the chilly winters can give tourists a feel of Himalayan regions while the warm breeze that also takes along with it sand and dust can give you a feel of the sandy breezes in Rajasthan. The climate of Delhi can be referred to as semi-arid and the summers and winters can be very extreme. The summers in Delhi start from the month of April and continue till the month of July. It is very hot and dry in the summer months, with temperature soaring up to 45 degree Celsius. The rainy season provides relief from searing heat, which is frequented by North West monsoon winds (North-west). It continues till the month of October. The winter months of December and January are characterized by dip in the temperature levels often reaching 5 degree Celsius to 0 degree Celsius. The months of October, November, February and March have pleasant weather and ideal for Tourism.

AGRICULTURE, STAPLE FOOD AND SOCIAL LIFE OF PEOPLE OF DELHI:

While the highest quality soil lies along the Yamuna, limited access to the river dictates that most agricultural production occurs along the periphery of the city. Approximately 7000 farmers reside along the shores of the Yamuna. The agriculture in Delhi can be categorized as rural and pre-urban agriculture. The rural farmers are mostly located on the periphery of the city of Delhi along the edges of the river and canals and grow major crops like sugarcane, wheat, jawar, bajra, pulses and paddy. The lands are big enough to grow these crops. In the pre-urban agriculture system, small farmers having small pieces of land scattered around the water beds in Delhi grow varieties of exotic crops that enhance their income to meet their essential and basic needs. These agricultural produce are very much economical and highly profitable as their target market is easily available in the cosmopolitan city. Major vegetables grown include cauliflower, cabbage, carrot, spinach, mustard (leaves), bottle gourd, bitter gourd, okra, brinjal, corn, tomato, watermelon, carrots, and radishes. In addition, culinary herbs such as thyme, rosemary, fenugreek and coriander are also cultivated. In addition to food crops, many farmers grow some type of flower, either roses or marigolds. Animal husbandry is an important component of the agriculture sector. The main livestock products are milk, eggs and meat. Farmers are involved in poultry farming and cattle rearing.

"The people of Delhi are generally referred as 'Delhi-ites' and they take the pride of falling in the fifth most populated urban area in the world and the people dwelling in this capital city - Delhi are regarded as the most hospitable people of India. They are friendly, cheerful and helpful. The inhabitants of Delhi honor their guests and treat them well with respect. As the inhabitants of Delhi hail from all parts of Indian region, the city is multi–ethnic, multi-cultured and multi-linguistic and most versatile cosmopolitan where formal caste and creed live together, which tends to influence the lifestyle and ideas. "

People here are engaged into different kinds of occupation, but take active part and share same platform and views every cultural and social gathering. Hinduism is the main religion followed by the people of Delhi and customs related mostly to this religion is followed. Apart from Hinduism the other commonly practiced religions here includes Islam, Sikhism and Christianity. Islam forms the second largest population after Hindus in New Delhi. The Muslim people of Delhi mainly live in Old Delhi in areas like Chandni Chowk, Daryaganj, and so on. There is no specific ethnic origin of the people of Delhi for most of them are migrants coming from other states opting for a better standard of living.

The city lifestyle in Delhi is also evident with the growing influx and modernization of Urban as well as Rural societies. One can witness a blend of modern lifestyles with the old customs and traditions in the people of Delhi. The people living in the area of Old Delhi still follow old traditions and customs whereas the people living in New Delhi follow new customs and traditions according to urbanization but still the people in both the area co-exist in harmony. The Sikhs never miss going to the Gurudwaras where we can get to enjoy the old Gurbhani, Kawwalis and the Prabhat Pheri. The Hindus strictly follow the traditional practices of aartis and bhajans. Delhi celebrates the traditional festival of 'Phoolwalo-Ki-Sair' with great joy. Other festivals celebrated by the Delhites are Diwali, Dusshera, Holi, Id-Ul-Fitr, Lohri, Mahavir Jayanti, Durga Puja, Lohri, Chhath, Krishna Janmastami, Maha Shivaratri, Eid ul-Fitr, Moharram, Christmas and Buddha Jayanti.

Earlier there were local markets in the city where people use to shop but with the change of lifestyle the way of shopping also changed. Now, Delhi has new shopping malls and complexes where people can get every kind of items as per their requirements. Apart of shopping Delhi is also famous for its numbers of restaurants and top class hotels one can get food of his/her own choice. Now world class hotels and restaurants can be found in each and every locality of Delhi, which indicates the changing lifestyle of the people. Young generation of the city loves to wear latest and trendy cloths while going to their colleges, market or out with their friends and family. According to western culture, the city is following modern lifestyle. Hindi is the official language of Delhi but for business and official purposes, English is generally used along with Urdu and Punjabi.

CHARACTERISTICS AND SALIENT FEATURES OF CUISINE:

Delhi, which has been a capital for several kingdoms in the past, has successfully adopted those flavors on its platter. It has been ruled successively by the Rajputs, Arabs, Afghanis, Mughals and the English, and even if those rulers do not exist in the city anymore, their cuisine is well preserved.

There is no specific food in the cuisine of the Delhiites for it is a place of amalgamation of several cuisine styles for people from different parts of the country came and settled in Delhi. The rich culinary heritage of the city is a mix of all those royal recipes from the Shahi kitchens of South India, Gujarat, Bengal, Rajasthan, Kashmir and the roadside stalls of chaats. The in-house family recipes passed down through generations and the plush restaurants that line the urban landscape of the city. These little pieces of history and culture clubbed together constitute what is known as the "**Dehlvi Cuisine**".

Slowly and gradually, Delhi assumed some of the aspects of the identity of all the types of people living in it, making multiple identities for itself. As a result, even the traditional food of New Delhi has no distinctiveness. Due to its proximity to Punjab and for which dominant Punjabi community recipes from Punjab are extremely popular in Delhi. Foods like Paneer Tikka, Tandoori chicken, Seekh, Boti kebab, Tandoori fish. Butter Chicken, Chole Bhature, Rajma Chawal, Saag and Makai Ki Roti, Tandoori Roti and Tandoori Chicken, Naans, Kormas, Pilafs and Nihari etc. and liberal doses of ghee, butter and cheese are savored with as much joy here as in Punjab.

However, as people of all communities, languages and creed have come to occupy a significant proportion of Delhi's population. Recipes from all corners of the country are gaining gradual yet notable popularity. Delhi happened to be the most favored and favorite city of Moghuls and hence the secrets of the rich and royal Mughlai food was handed down to the people of this city. Delhi takes pride to have inherited the recipes deemed 'fit for royals'. For, it consists of a superb mix of aromatic spices, exotic sausages, butter based curries, loads of dry fruits and roasted meats cooked in earthen ovens called tandoors. In Delhi one can see a Punjabi enjoying idlli and sambhar whereas a South Indian eating Chole Bhature. With globalization, the Delhiites enjoy the best of embrace the best of the Indian and International cuisines which includes authentic Chinese, Thai, Lebanese, Israeli, Japanese, Spanish, Italian, Spanish, Mediterranean, French, Moroccan, Swiss or American food. So depending on our taste preferences, there is a specific cuisine for everyone.

Deluxe and five-star hotels, exclusive and popular restaurants scattered all over Delhi, and the busy dhabas (the humble Indian forerunners of modern restaurants) provide fare that would tempt the most fastidious of Nawabs (noblemen) or gourmets living in times when the culinary arts had reached a peak and feasts had become a measure of class, style and social status. Delhi offers a whole gamut of eating joints in the form of low budget restaurants, elite restaurants and road side Dhabas that satiate your taste buds with authentic Delhi cuisine. The one exclusive feature however about Delhi eating joints is that the capital city has a several streets and lanes that are totally dedicated to food. Some of the popular road side eateries in Delhi include places like Chandni Chowk, Paranthe wali gali, Annapoorna, Ghantewala, Bengali Market, Greater Kailash and Sunder Nagar are famous for entertaining their gastronomes with kababs, rotis chaat, bhelpuri, sweetmeats and biryani. For example, Chandni Chowk area of the city boasts of the most delicious paranthas (a sort of bread). Then, there is the Bengali Market in New Delhi that is very popular for Chaat Papri, Golgappas, Sweets, etc.

Delhi is also very popular for its roadside vendors that serve awesome local cuisine. However, before eating make sure that the place is neat, clean and hygienic. Whatever one feels like having, the choices are wide. Mughlai, Chinese, Continental, food from the Northwest Frontier, South Indian food, delicacies from the coastal states of India, a variety of salads, fast-food creations, piping hot Punjabi makki ki rotis (flat bread prepared from corn) and sarson ka saag (prepared from fresh, green mustard leaves), bar-be-cued sizzlers, Turkish delights, the unusual flavors of cuisine perfected in beautiful Kashmir, Tibetan food, dishes from Japan-one just has to name it and it shall served, for, in matters of taste. Savories, snacks, biscuits, sweets, paneer, spices, vegetables and fruits – everything is available in old Delhi. Delhi offers the same, virtually unlimited choice as did Aladdin's lamp.

With the introduction of centralized malls and shopping complexes in the past few years, food cultures have blended in even more. Most eateries offer multiple cuisines at their service nowadays. You can feed your taste buds with South Indian dishes like Dosa, Idli, Sambar to Italian dishes like pasta, to North Indian dishes like Dal Makhani, Paneer curries, and Naan.

Famous traveler, Marco Polo recalls that kebabs were served during the Delhi Sultanate and was enjoyed by the royalty and commoners alike. Some of the famous Kebabs are Boti Kebab, Shami Kebab, Kathi Kebab etc. Another Mughlai dish, Nihari, which was prepared in the royal kitchens of the Mughals for breakfast is now a popular dish among the people of all the classes. Biryani, a meat based rice dish was a favorite of the Mughal emperors and is enjoyed all over India today. This entire specialty makes Delhi stand apart in terms of food culture. It is unique and wondrous in itself. People still wonder why the capital is called "**Delhi-Belly**"?

POPULAR FOODS AND SPECIALTIES:

Chittaranjan Park- CR Park houses the maximum number of Bengalis in Delhi. Today, the Bengali food at CR park is exactly what one would expect to get in the City of Joy (Kolkata), with many specialty Bengali dishes and ingredients available easily. Be it a mustard mixed Shorshe eelish (Hilsa fish), or mishti doi, or jhal muri and mochar chop, CR Park has outlets selling all these and more. It is, in-fact, a great source for all sorts of ingredients for Bengali cooking, right from the spices to fresh fish. Culturally too, it's a mini Bengal. In Delhi, this is usually a go-to place for a taste of Bengal. Crispy-spicy Kolkata styled puchkas unlike Delhi's gol gappa, puchka has its own charm, it's crispier, it's spicy, the stuffing is how it should be - potatoes mixed with spices and a lot of chillies, and the paani is a sour mixture of tamarind, lemon and everything Bengali. All type of Bengali snacks such as Jhalmuri (an uncooked mixture made of puffed rice, onions, spices, peanuts and a lot of other ingredients depending on individual tastes. The usual options are boiled potatoes, tomatoes, finely sliced coconut, mustard oil and roasted gram), Chur mur (Typical Bengali chaat) Matar ghugunee (yellow peas cooked in thick gravy), deepfried, pocketsized, goldenbrown cutlets, aloo chop (spiced mashed potatoes besan batter fried), piyazy (onion slices besan batter fried), Beguni (sliced eggplant coated in besan and deep fried), Fish fingers, Egg devil (boiled egg coated in besan and deep fried), Mutton cutlet, Mocha chop (banana flower cutlet), Posto narekel bora (fritters made of poppy seeds and coconut). Mughlai parotha (Mughlai-style stuffed bread), Kolkata Hot Kathi Roll (a skewer-roasted kebab wrapped in a paratha bread,) are only some of the names of the unique offerings that are difficult to find outside of Kolkata. This place also serves other gastronomical delights such as honey chili potato and tandoori chicken and many other Continental and Chinese cuisines. Apart from this other eating joints include Karim's, Sanjha Chula, a chaap outlet and other north-indian cuisine joints. However sign boards of "luchi aloo" (aloo curry and puri), Kosha Mangsho (spicy Bengali styled mutton), Bhat (boiled rice) and Doi katla (fish prepared in curd which is tangy soft and moist from the inside), Bhetki shorsha (a unique dish where the fish is boiled in milk first and spiced and oiled later). If prepared well, it has a creamy, runny flavor in each bite, with an interesting sprinkle of the pungent taste of the mustard oil that's been used. Order a slice of Beguni (sliced eggplant coated in besan and deep fried) as a side.

Connaught Place- Connaught place is the hub for all people whether local or foreigners for hangouts. It is New Delhi's central business area and is famous for sampling some street food or fine dining. Its Cha Bar is the first of its kind urban contemporary space that has history of 90 years where people can enjoy two of the best things in life: food and books. The restaurant is an extension of the neighboring Oxford Bookstore and visitors can browse for books here while waiting for their food order from the varied menu. Berco's restaurant offers Chinese and Thai offerings and is perfect for a family lunch or dinner. Their variety of dishes ensures that there's something for everyone, and the reasonable prices allow you to eat guilt free. One of the most distinguished names when it comes to Chinese and Thai cuisines, they have a well-curated menu of dishes, which are prepared only by the qualified chef using the finest quality of ingredients, so that each bite you take feels as perfect as the last. Saravana Bhavan - high-quality South Indian Vegetarian restaurant in Delhi has long been known as a vegetarian's paradise. Their wide range of dosas and other South Indian delights including Tamil Nadu Thali will leave you spoilt for choice. It's one of the best places to eat after a great shopping session at Janpath market. Mother India- restaurant has the same name as a 1957 Bollywood movie. The extensive menu consists of more than 150 dishes from across the country.

The kebabs are popular here. However, ideally be adventurous and try some of the lesser-known specialty dishes such as grilled river fish marinated with raja mirchi from Nagaland, home-style Mandi chicken curry from Himachal Pradesh, or mutton (goat) curry from Odisha. Rajdhani- restaurants serves the best of its kind of Gujrati and Rajasthani thali. If you are carved to sea-food, you can visit the famous Lady Baga restaurant which serves the original Goan cuisine, which serves Bibinka, Goan fish curry, Sorpetal, prawn curry. Moreover you can find burgers, snacks, and some very creative cocktails on their menu. The Smoke House Deli offers best kind of continental dishes Peri Peri Chicken, Caesar salad, or a tenderloin steak. Top it off with one of the fruit and herb infused martinis, or artisanal cocktails. The Masala Trail by Osama Jalali serves Gujarati savouries to Banarasi Chaats like Bedmi Puri, Chaat, Gini Dosa, Dabeli, Haji Ali Fruit Cream. The street foods include Kachori with aloo ki sabzi served by a vendor at Hanuman mandir, Chole bhature from Jain Chawal wale, Momos, Kathi Roll & Paneer Ball at Deepauls.

Dilli Haat- Dilli Haat is an open air food plaza and craft bazaar managed by the DTTDC (Delhi Tourism and Transportation Development Corporation). It was initially established to provide a platform to all the craftsmen who come to Delhi from all over the country. All these craftsmen are from small towns and villages with limited access and this helped in giving them a platform where they could showcase their art to the rest of the world. The Dilli Haat is the only place that offers variety in food. The food comprises of cuisine from all over the states of India. The dishes range from different states of India like Awadh Cuisine (Shami, Galauti, Boti and Tangri Kebabs,

Dum Biryani) Uttrakhand Cuisine (Kafli, Pahari urad Dal, Meat Bhat, Rhododendron), Wazwan Cuisine (Rista, Gushtaba, Haksaag), Meghalaya Cuisine (Doh Neiiong, Doh Syiar Khleh, Wak Bijak), Arunachal Pradesh or Momo-mia Cuisine(Dimsums, Thukpa), Behari or Mahak Cuisine (Litti Choka, Madua Roti Saag), Rajasthan Cuisine (Khoya Kachori, Besangatta), Manipur Cuisine (Erombadish, Prawn Pakora, Tarai Thong, Ngou Thon), Odisha Cuisine (Prawn Masala, Crab Sizzler and Katahchaatthat (for vegetarians)), Kerala Cuisine (Aapam, Idiyappam, Chicken and Meat Stew), Hyderabadi Cuisine (Handi Biryani, ChickenChangezi, Double Ka meetha),Tamil Nadu Cuisine (Dosa, Sambhar, Payasam kheer), Bengali Cuisine (Fish Thali, Sandesh), Nagaland Cuisine (Prawn sizzlers), Maharashtra Cuisine (PavBhaji, Masala Bhel, Vadapav), Assam Cuisine (Fish Curry, Luci Bhaj, Narikolpitha). At Dilli Haat one can increase his taste bud with different variety of dishes that too at decent price.

Hudson Lane- Hudson Lane and Vijay Nagar have become a hotbed of cafes and restaurants in the past few years for both students and families. From Italian and Mexican to Moroccan, Marathi and Rajasthani to Manipuri and Naga, North Indian to South Indian and Chinese and Korean to Tibetan and Bhutanese, this place has become a gastronomical hotspot never ceasing to amaze its inhabitants. Breakfast at the DDA (Delhi development authority) market is quintessentially north-Indian. The options vary from soft _melt-in-the mouth' Rajma Chawal with its a distinct aroma that entices from a mile away, to heavily stuffed paranthas. Everything has to be followed by strong "masala chai". A left from DDA Market and a few steps towards the NDPL Office, Shagun is famous for serving authentic Chinese fare since 2011. It is immensely popular for its Single/Double person Jumbo platters, so a lunch here is a must. A typical platter consists of starters - a healthy and flavor-some soup (either Sweet Corn or Manchow) and a choice of either dumplings (fried/ steamed and heavily stuffed) or won-tons as starters. This is followed by either Fried rice or Hakka noodles, depending on what you prefer, accompanied by perfectly balanced and succulent Chili Chicken or Chicken Manchurian (non-vegetarian) as the main course. A few paces from Shagun, the Big Yellow Door greets a line of customers queuing to get inside. Sometimes, it takes half an hour to get a table indicating how hugely popular it has become since it opened its doors in 2013. The soft, silky and creamy white sauce Arrabiata pasta, the immensely tender patty of the Chicken Juicy Burger and the crunchy Mexican Nachos. Bake Lane is a tiny place with old English style ambiance and fragrant smell of freshly baked cinnamon rolls coming out from the chimney serves soft and buttery pastries with piping hot coffee. Creamy Crème Brulee and Banoffee pie are personal favorites. Mr. Crust Bakers offers some of the finest bakery products since 2010. Sweet and buttery croissants that melt at first bite, freshly baked thick-crust Apple Pie, soft and creamy red velvet cupcakes, subtly tangy Lemon Tarts, hot doughnuts, fresh fruit pudding, delicious birthday cakes and pastries with numerous flavors along with savory dishes such as thick-crust double-decker cheese pizza, spicy mushroom plait, wholesome brown bread club sandwiches are the favourites. The Organic Kitchen serves proper 'ghar ka khana' meal for one to feel right at home. Kanglei Fast Food- „Kanglei" is the historic name of Manipur, offers the traditional Manipuri dishes like Hot and pungent Eromba (mashed potatoes with dried fish), King Chilly (succulent Pork curry cooked with sour bamboo shoots, sweet and creamy), Ooti (lentils cooked with soda), tangy Fish curry and more.

Jama Masjid- The adjoining area of this place has become the paradise for food connoisseurs. The lane opposite Jama Masjid - Bazar Matia Mahal is filled with heady aromas from big heaps of Keema samosas, vats of buffalo biryani, grilling botis and kebabs and hot paneer jalebi. To cool down, there are drums filled with Rooh Afza sherbet and dishes of dahi vada. Kallan Sweets started by Mohd. Shaan in 1939 is famous for its fresh batch of sweets and snacks. One of their specialties is the bright orange and thick paneer ki jalebi, which uses a cottage cheese paste in lieu of much of the flour that goes into the more common jalebi. It is extremely popular in Ramzan, along with other festive delicacies such as khoya samosa, keema samosa (shaped like gujiya and stuffed with minced meat) and paneer ke pakode. Haji Mohd. Hussain Fried Chicken established 40 years ago, this shop has been dishing out fried chicken in Delhi and served with rumali roti, onions and special tangy masala chutney. During Ramzan, Haji sa'ab also sells keema goli, which are small balls made out of minced meat, and served with onion and chutney. Kebabs at Qureshi, Lallu Kebabi, Bhaijaan and Kale Baba are known kebabchi famous for seekh and boti kebabs. All of them make excellent kebabs of buffalow smeared with butter, onions, and spicy chutney. They also sell more than 350 varieties of dates, including the ones dipped in chocolate, honey, pista & even apricot. Bhaijaan Kebabs in Chitli Qabar sells fibrous shammi kebabs deep fried in oil. Another kebab shop in Sui Walan, Kale Baba ke Kebabs, is popular for their sutli kebabs - these are so soft, they have to be held together with a twine of thread. Sutli kebabs are served on a green leaf, with radish and mint chutney. Changezi Chicken established in 1986 is the signature dish served in a tangy gravy of yogurt, tomatoes and onion. They also prepare beef biryani, paya, nahari and a multitude of other chicken preparations. Laung Churey Kebab sells something that vegetarians are delighted by: laung churey kebab, made from besan, aata and onion. There are three varieties - fried, kebabs which are soaked in water after frying and long vegetarian seekhs, all of which are made in a small shop nearby. These kebabs are served with chutney of red chillies, amchur, and salt and garam masala. Karim"s especialises in Chicken Jehangiri and Mutton Burra. Twenty five years old Cool Point is famous for its shahi tukda and phirni. It is also known for its kesar milk, badammilk, lassi and mango and vanilla ice cream. Ameer Sweet House serves the best like keema and khoya samosa, balushahi, besan ke laddu, chamcham and gulaab jamun apart from chhole bhature and pakoras. Gur ka Sharbat at Pahadi Imli opened in 1947 serves jaggary sharbat along with other indigenous made mock-tails.

Karol Bagh-This area is famous for its Punjabi delicacies, constantly bustling with activity, culinary aromas and pleasures. Roshan Di Kulfi is probably the most famous eating joint of Karol Baghserving various Indian snacks. The famous kulfi faluda is served with colored, sweet vermicelli. Changezi second most visited restaurant in Karol Bagh has made a reputation for itself with its array of Mughlai food. If you are a non-vegetarian, Changezi could be your next best favorite joint to have butter chicken and Nalli Nihari with some hot Tandoori Naan. Peshawari

Chicken Corner serves delicious roasted chicken, Soya Malai Chaap and the best Kaali Mirch Chicken. Sandoz serves Mughlai, Chinese and North Indian food and the best one is theirs Chicken Korma. Suruchi is a 100% pure vegetarian restaurant dealing specifically in Gujarati and Rajasthani Cuisinealong with North Indian, Punjabi and even a South Indian Thali. The three decade old Om Corner Chhole Bhature is definitely one of Delhi's best chole bhature joints. Art of Spices prepares classic tawa rolls or delicious tandoori preparations especially Malai Tikka Roll and Cream Chicken.

Nizamuddin - Hazrat Nizamuddin's Dargah, considered one of the last great Sufi abodes is also a haven for carnivorous street food delights like kebabs, tikkas, nihari and more. The Dargah itself can be accessed by three alleyways, all lined with Mughlai eateries serving some of the most exquisite naharis, keema, roganjosh and of course kebabs. Moradabad Ki Mashhoor Biryani Ki Puraani Dukaan serves the best biriyanis of Delhi. Manpasand Nahari Roti Waale especialises in Nahari alongwith hot, soft and yeasty khameeri rotis. Ghalib Kebab Corner especialises in shaami kebab chicken tikka and mutton tikka. Al Quresh serves the best tangdi kebabs with green chutney. The two curries—the chicken qorma and the karahi chicken are also best sold. Kit Care Kabab Corner- prepares varieties of mouthwatering kebabs and tikkas apart from Dahi Butter Chicken or the Mast enjoyed with soft roomali roti. Nasir-is famous for its silver foiled covered Kheer with a hint of cardamom in it.

Paharganj- Paharganj in New Delhi is a land mark of street food like Parathas. Kulchas and Chat. Sita Ram Diwan Chand is the right place for delicious Chole Bhature, along-with onions, pickle and green chillies and varieties of chat and mouthwatering pani-puri. Chawla Ke Mashoor Special Naan serve especial Naans. Their Chur-Chur Naan Thali are quite popular. They serve four kinds of Thali - Aloo Pyaaz Chur-Chur Naan Thali, Stuff Paneer Chur-Chur Naan Thali, Special Chur-Chur Naan Thali and Plain Naan Thali. The Thali comes with 2 Butter Naan, Chholey, Mix Daal and Raita. Multani Geela Kulche Wala- serves flavorful Multani food in Paharganj. They are famous for their Geela Kulcha. Unlike the regular Kulcha, Geela Kulcha is broken into small pieces and smeared into the Multani Chholey. The Kulcha is soaked in Chhole and then topped with a load of tangy imli ki chutney and green chutney. It has a very unique taste, a perfect combination of sweet and tangy flavours. Shri Baanke Bihari Samosa Wala- This legendary shop in Paharganj Market is immensely famous for its Samosas, Gulab Jamuns and Kachoris.

SPECIALTIES DURING FESTIVALS AND OTHER OCCASIONS:

Everyone in Delhi loves eating. Walk into any wedding, party or social occasion and you will see huge tables groaning under an astonishing array of mouth watering – and sometimes nose-watering too – dishes emanating exquisite aromas and fragrance. Usually, in the Delhi social scene, a perfunctory 'hello' is followed by the hostess indicating to the guest where the food has been laid; just what the guest had been too polite to ask himself but was, of course, dying to know.

"An indifferent table is social suicide. On the other hand, feed a Delhiite well and you've got a friend for life; on a full stomach he will give you even unto half

his kingdom. And what's more, being a thorough generous live-for-today Delhite, won't even regret it the morning after. Perhaps that is why Delhi is the restaurant capital of India, just like Mumbai and Bangalore are the discothèque and pub hubs respectively. The city is crawling with restaurants of all variety, nationality and vintage."

Delhi's famed cuisine has evolved as a result of centuries of different ruling empires & the confluence of varied cultures in the capital. Be the rich Mughlai or Frontier Cuisine, age-old eateries and street food of Old Delhi to the Chinese food vans and new age specialty restaurants, Delhi is a foodie's paradise.

Delhi is the city of historical landmarks. Everything from Asoka-era iron pillars to Mughal forts to the haunting tombs of the various invaders who held sway over Delhi for shorter or longer periods to the massive Purana Qila (Old Fort) which is said to date back to the time of the Mahabharata can be found here.

And all of them have left the taste of their food behind. Take the "gol gappa," the tasty balls of fried dough filled with savory water, tangy chutneys and an assortment of texture differentiators from tiny slices of boiled potatoes or peas to pomegranate seeds. While any vendor on Delhi's streets will supply you with a plate, in some parts of old Delhi where the Nawabi influence of Lucknow lingers, you will get "batashas" – the same, yet subtly different. And in the newer parts and malls, you can even get the Mumbai version, "pani puri."

Dehlvi is an Urdu word which roughly translates to "From Delhi". Delhi's cuisine is a mix of Indo-Persian culinary traits brought in by Mughals, the European and various refugee settlements who came from different parts of the country.

Think Old Delhi, and you are immediately transported to the lanes of loaded paranthas, succulent kababs, and absolutely sinful sweetmeats.

The Lutyen's Delhi has its own vintage charm tracing back to the colonial roots and their culinary masterpieces.

The Punjabis gave the city its widely acclaimed Dal Makhani, Tandoori Chicken and Butter Chicken. Similarly, the Kolkata Kathi Rolls, Mughlai Parothas, Fish cutlets and the Ghugni of the Bengali settlement in CR Park and the Dosas, Idiappams and Utthapams of the South Indian inhabitants further add to the richness of the local cuisine of Delhi. It is no wonder then that the capital is also often dubbed as the culinary capital of the nation.

The confluence of cultures witnessed by the city merits a chronicle of its own. Delhi, which has been a capital for several kingdoms in the past, has successfully adopted those flavors on its platter. The same goes for all the migrated communities who came, settled and made Delhi their own. The rich culinary heritage of the city is a mix of all those royal recipes from the Shahi kitchens, and the roadside chaats, the in-house family recipes passed down through generations and the plush restaurants that line the urban landscape of the city. These little pieces of history and culture clubbed together constitute what is known as the Dehlvi Cuisine.

When you are in Old Delhi, you just can't miss the food there. The streets buzz with activity and are filled with the aroma of food. For the connoisseurs, there are restaurants like Karim's. For the food historians, there's a chance to taste Butter Chicken at Moti Mahal.

Chandni Chowk, often called the food capital of India, is famous for its street food. The variety consists of snacks, especially chaat. If you wish to enjoy it, shed your high-brow attitude to soak in the flavours and delicacies. Chandni Chowk resembles a fair every day. The streets are lined with halwais (sweet-sellers), namkeenwallahs (sellers of savouries) and paranthe-wallahs (sellers of rich, flaky breads soaked in ghee). Though the number of shops in this lane has reduced - one wonders if their owners are more interested in McDonald's franchises - there still are a few left from the good old days. The paranthas are fried in pure ghee in cast-iron pans. They are served with Mint Chutney, Banana - Tamarind Chutney, vegetable pickle and Aloo Subzi.

Half a century back, you could get only a few varieties - Aloo Parantha, Gobhi Parantha and Matar Parantha, stuffed with potato, cauliflower and peas respectively. While these continue to be the most popular, there are several new variants. These include lentils, fenugreek, radish, papad, carrot and mixed. Besides, there are paranthas which cost slightly more and include those stuffed with paneer, mint, lemon, chilly, dry fruits, cashew, raisins, almond, rabdi, khurchan, banana, karela, lady's finger and tomato.

The real flavour of the Delhi street food lies in the chaat. The original chaat is a mixture of potato pieces, crispy fried bread, Dahi Bhalla, gram and tangy-salty spices. The mixture is garnished with sour home-made Indian chilly and saunth (dried ginger and tamarind sauce), fresh green coriander leaves and yoghurt. However, there are several other popular variants now, including the one with an Aloo Tikki.

Gol Gappe served with a type of Jal Jeera that's packed with harad (a digestive), kachoris stuffed with potato and peas, Gobhi-Matar Samosas, Dahi Bhalla and Matar Paneer Tikki are the fastest-selling items here.

Fruit Chaat that has become a quintessential part of the sounds and sights of Chandni Chowk. Though they do offer a version of Pao Bhaji and Aloo Tikki, it's the Fruit Chaat that is the winner here. Dahi Bhalla need not always be a part of chaat. The delicacy called Dahi Bhalla is a deep-fried urad dal dumpling smothered in whipped curd. Often, it is streaked with chocolate brown laces of sweet-sour tamarind chutney. Pink pomegranate seeds glisten in the folds of the curd.

Kachori, usually stuffed with pulses and served with potato curry, is another delicacy that makes your mouth water. Perhaps the most famous is Urad Dal Kachori, which is served with Aloo Subzi.

On the sweeter side, Rabdi Faluda is a must. Apart from standard ice creams, they also serve milkshakes, fruit shakes, ice-cream shakes and sundaes. If you are interested in kulfi - a flavoured frozen dessert made of milk - venture towards the Ajmeri Gate. What you get here is kulfi as kulfi should be - sinful, scrumptious and oh-so-splendid! Order any flavour - Kesar, Pista, Rose, Kewra, Banana, Mango, or Pomegranate.

Coming back to Chandni Chowk, you meet the Old and Famous Jalebiwala. Refresh yourself with a delicious plate of hot jalebis - a sweet made by deepfrying batter in a kind of pretzel shape and then soaked in syrup. Also, don't miss the Jama Masjid area that buzzes with activity. The aroma of food wafts to your nose from the Urdu Bazaar facing Gate No. 1 of the Masjid and a side street called Matia Mahal. The smell of fresh fish, aromatic kebabs and fried chicken is in the air. Vendors sell kebabs and tikkas (made of buffalo meat) wrapped in rumali roti (paper-thin bread) at throwaway prices.

The Mutton Burrahs here are easily the best in the city. They are practically the only place to serve Nihari and Paaya. Other un-miss-ables are Stew, Mutton Korma, Shammi Kabab and Shahjahani Korma.

Ghantewala at Chandni Chowk is more than 200 years old. The sweets here are prepared in pure desi ghee. Highly recommended are the Sohan Halwa Papdi, Pista Samosa and Badam Burfi - truly sinful pieces of heaven on earth.

After all these years, the Tandoori Chicken is still succulent. Chor Bizarre is one of the few restaurants to serve Kashmiri food and attempts to replicate a 'thieves market' in its decor. Specially recommended for non-vegetarians is the Tabak Maaz. Also good are the Yakhni, Rishta and Goshtaba, besides the wonderful greens - Haaq.

*"**BUTTER CHICKEN IN DELHI**: Butter Chicken originated at the Moti Mahal, Darya Ganj in the 1950s. The restaurant was famous for its Tandoori Chicken. The cooks there would recycle the chicken juices that were left over by adding butter and tomato. Once, be it by chance or by design, this sauce was tossed around with pieces of Tandoori Chicken. And the rest is history. Butter Chicken was born and soon set tongues drooling the world over. Butter Chicken is creamy with thick, red tomato gravy. It tastes slightly sweet. The sauce percolates into the chicken pieces, making them soft and juicy. This melt-in-mouth dish tastes best with tandoori roti or naan."*

FESTIVITIES:

India International Trade Fair - India International Trade Fair or the IITF is an annual fair that takes place at the grounds of Pragati Maidan. Organized by the India Trade Promotion Organization (ITPO) takes place in November and provides a good platform to the manufacturers, traders, exporters and importers of the country to showcase their products.

Surajkund Crafts Mela - Surajkund Crafts Mela is held at Surajkund - near Delhi in the month of February for two weeks. Artists, painters, weavers, sculptors and craftsmen from all over the country participate in the fair.

Phoolwalon Ki Sair - Phoolwalon ki Sair festival meaning Procession of Flower Sellers, takes place in the Mehrauli. An annual event, it consists of a procession taken out by flower sellers down the flower-seller's promenade.

Mango Festival – The Mango Festival is organized in the month of July and held at the Talkatora stadium and also at the Delhi Haats. This festival presents one with as many as almost 500 varieties of the king of fruits.

Qutub Festival - Qutub Festival is organized at Qutub Minar during Sharad Purnima (October-November). A classical music and dance extravaganza, it lasts for three days. Some of the most graceful and elegant performers can be seen dancing to the music here.

Recipes from Delhi:

Shami Kebabs

Ingredients

- 500 Gram Mutton Keema
- ½ Cup Chana Dal
- 2 TbspGhee
- 1 Cinnamon Stick
- 1 Mace
- 3 Cloves
- 1 Bay Leaf
- 2 Green Cardamoms
- 7 Black Peppercorns
- 1 Brown Cardamom
- ½ tsp Salt
- ½ tsp Red Chilli Powder
- 1 Cup Water
- 1 Onion
- 1 Green Chilli
- ½ Lemon

Method

- How to Make Mutton Shami Kebab
- In a bowl soak ½ cup of chana dal for 30 minutes.Mutton Shami Kebab
- Heat 2 tbspghee in a pressure cooker. Add cinnamon stick, mace, cloves, bay leaf, green cardamoms, black peppercorns and brown cardamom. Mix them thoroughly.Mutton Shami Kebab
- When they crackle add mutton Keema to it.Mutton Shami Kebab
- Now add salt and red chilli powder.Mutton Shami Kebab
- Mix it thoroughly and cook for a minute.
- Add soaked chana dal and mix it well by adding a cup of water.Mutton Shami Kebab

- Pressure cook the mixture until the mutton gets soft.Mutton Shami Kebab
- After 1-2 whistles remove the cover and mix it well.
- If water remains, cook till the mutton dries up.Mutton Shami Kebab
- 10.Grind and then refrigerate for 30 minutes to get a thick paste.Mutton Shami Kebab
- Mix onion, green chilli and lime juice to this paste and mix thoroughly.Mutton Shami Kebab
- Make flat balls out of this dough and refrigerate for another 10 minutes.Mutton Shami Kebab
- Heat a tbspof ghee in another pan and shallow fry the kebabs from all sides until golden brown.Mutton Shami Kebab
- Place them on an absorbent paper and serve hot.

Matar Paneer

Ingredients

For onion tomato paste:

- 2 tbspoil
- 1 onion, sliced
- 3 clove garlic, chopped
- 1 inch ginger
- 3 tomato, sliced

Other Ingredients:

- 2 tbspoil

- 1 bay leaf
- 1 inch cinnamon stick
- 2 pods cardamom
- 1 tsp cumin / jeera
- ¼ tsp turmeric
- 1 tsp kashmiri red chilli powder
- 1 tbspbesan / gram flour
- ¼ tsp cumin powder
- 1 tsp coriander powder
- 1 tsp salt
- 1 cup water
- 1 cup peas / matar
- 12 cubes paneer / cottage cheese
- 2 tbspcoriander, finely chopped
- ¼ tsp garam masala
- 1 tsp kasuri methi, crushed

Method

- In a large kadai heat 2 tbspoil and saute spices.
- Add ¼ tsp turmeric, 1 tsp chilli powder and 1 tbspbesan. Roast well.
- Add in prepared onion tomato paste and saute well.
- Further add ¼ tsp cumin powder, 1 tsp coriander powder and 1 tsp salt.
- Now add 1 cup water and stir well.
- Add in 1 cup peas and stir well. Cover and cook for 10 minutes.
- Add in 12 cubes paneer and simmer for 10 minutes.
- Now add 2 tbspcoriander, ¼ tsp garam masala and 1 tsp kasuri methi.
- Finally, enjoy matar paneer with roti or rice.

Chicken Kandhari Kofta

Ingredients

- Chicken Mince 400 grams
- Cashewnut paste ½ teaspoon
- Salt to taste
- Oil 3 tablespoons
- Onion paste boiled ¾ cup
- Ginger-garlic paste 1 tablespoon
- Red chilli powder 1 teaspoon
- Tomato puree ½ cup
- Cashewnut paste ¼cup
- Garam masala powder ½ teaspoon
- Fresh cream 2 tablespoons

Method

- Mix cinnamon powder, one tea spoon salt and chicken mince thoroughly. Divide this mixture into twelve equal portions. Shape them into balls and place on a greased baking tray. Refrigerate for thirty minutes and then cook in a preheated oven for fifteen minutes.
- Heat oil in a pan. Add boiled onion paste and cook till onions turn pink. Add ginger garlic paste and red chilli powder. Sauté for a minute on a low heat. Stir in tomato puree and cashewnut paste dissolved in a little water. Cook for five minutes, stirring constantly. Add one and half cups of water, bring it to a boil. Add cooked chicken koftas, garam masala powder and pomegranate syrup. Correct seasoning. Simmer for five minutes.
- Finish with fresh cream and serve hot.

Dal Maharani

Ingredients
For pressure cooking:

- ¾ cup black urad dal, soaked overnight
- 2 tbsprajma, soaked overnight
- 4 cup water
- 1 tsp oil

Other Ingredients:

- 1 tbspbutter
- 1 tsp oil
- 1 tsp cumin / jeera
- 1 bay leaf
- 2 pods cardamom / elachi
- 2 tsp kasuri methi
- 1 onion, finely chopped
- 1 tsp ginger garlic paste
- 1 chilli, slit
- ¼ tsp turmeric
- ¾ tsp kashmiri red chilli powder
- ½ tsp garam masala
- 1½ cup tomato puree
- 1 tsp salt
- 2 tbspcream
- 2 tbspcoriander, finely chopped For tempering:
- 1 tsp butter
- 3 clove garlic, sliced
- Pinch kashmiri red chilli powder

Method

- Firstly, in a large kadai heat 1 tbspbutter and 1 tsp oil.
- Add in 1 tsp cumin, 1 bay leaf, 2 pods cardamom and 2 tsp kasuri methi. Saute until the spices turn aromatic.
- Further add 1 onion, 1 tsp ginger garlic paste and 1 chilli.
- Saute until the onions turn golden brown.
- Keeping the flame on low, add ¼ tsp turmeric, ¾ tsp chilli powder, ½ tsp garam masala.
- Now add 1½ cup tomato puree. To prepare tomato puree blend 3 large tomatoes to a smooth paste.
- Add in cooked dal, 1 tsp salt and mix well.
- Simmer for 20 minutes stirring in between to prevent from burning.
- Now add 2 tbspcream, 2 tbspcoriander and mix well.
- Pour the tempering over the dal and enjoy dal maharani with jeera rice.

Tawa Pulao

Ingredients

- 4 cups boiled and cooled rice *
- 1 tablespoon oil
- 1 tablespoon butter
- 2-3 tablespoon water
- 4 -5 medium sized tomatoes finely chopped
- 1 onion finely chopped
- 3-4 grated garlic
- 1 carrot diced /chopped
- 1 /2 cup chopped bell pepper

- ½ cup green peas boiled /steamed
- 1 tablespoon red chilly powder
- 1 tablespoon pav bhaji masala
- Salt to taste
- Good squeeze of fresh lemon
- Fistful of fresh coriander chopped

Method

- Heat oil and butter in a heavy bottom non stick pan
- Add the onion and sauté till lightly browned.
- Add grated garlic and carrots.
- Saute until carrots are a bit tender.
- Add chopped tomatoes and salt.
- Sauté till tomatoes become tender.
- Add in the chopped bell peppers Add pav bhaji masala, red chilly powder .
- Let it cook for 2 minutes.
- Add water if needed.
- Add in steamed / boiled green peas . Cook for a minute.
- Add the rice and give it a nice mix until the masala is coated well.
- Taste test and add lemon juice .
- Adjust seasoning as per your preference if needed.
- Cook the rice for 2 more minutes.
- Fold in some chopped cilantro .
- Serve hot with a side of chilled cucumber raita and some papad.

Gajar aur khajoor ka halwa

Ingredients

- 1 tbspghee
- 8-10 cashew nuts
- 3 cups carrots ,washed, peeled and grated
- ¼ cup sugar
- 2 cups full-fat milk
- ¾ cup dates ,de-seeded and chopped
- 8-10 golden raisins
- 2 tsp green cardamom powder

Method

- Heat ghee in a kadhai or thick bottomed pan. Add cashew nuts and lightly roast them for a minute or two.
- Remove the cashew nuts and keep aside.
- In the same pot, add the grated carrots and sugar. Mix well and cook for about 5 mins.
- Add milk and continue to cook on medium flame for another 15 mins till there is a boil in the milk and the milk starts to reduce.
- Add dates, raisins, cardamom powder and mix. Cook for another 10 minutes with occasional stirring until all the milk has evaporated and the carrot halwa is thick.
- Serve hot or cold.

Paneer Taash Kabab

Ingredients

- Cottage Cheese 400 grams
- Mint Chutney cut into rings 2 medium
- Tomatoes cut into rings 2 medium
- Mint chutney 8 tablespoons

- Cheese 8 slices
- Fresh cream 1 tablespoon
- Cheese grated 1 cup
- Peppercorns crushed ½ teaspoon
- For marinade
- Hung yogurt 1/3 cup
- Red chilli powder 2 teaspoons Coriander powder 1 teaspoon
- Cumin powder 1 teaspoon
- Ginger-garlic paste 4 teaspoons
- Garam masala powder 1 teaspoon
- Mustard oil 2 tablespoons
- Chaat masala to taste
- Salt to taste

Method

- Preheat oven to 180°C. Slice the paneer into seven slices.
- Mix well all the marinade ingredients and spread evenly on the paneer slices. Set aside for ten minutes.
- Spread mint chutney evenly on the paneer slices. Arrange onion and tomato slices on each paneer slice and cover with the cheese slice.
- Stack each paneer slice with its layers one on top of the other, by repeating the process.
- Make a mixture of cream, grated cheese and crushed peppercorns and pour over the top layer.
- Place the last cheese slice on top, bake at 180°C for ten minutes in the oven.
- Cut equally into pieces of desired shape.

Chicken Hazaarvi

Ingredients

- Boneless chicken cut into 1 inch cubes 250 grams
- Ginger-garlic paste 1 tablespoon
- Salt to taste
- Black pepper powder ½ teaspoon
- Processed cheese ½ cup
- Green chilli finely chopped 1
- Fresh coriander leaves finely chopped 2 tablespoons
- Mace powder ½ teaspoon
- Nutmeg powder ½ teaspoons
- Egg 1
- Fresh cream 2 tablespoons
- Butter for basting

Method

- Preheat oven at 180ºC. Spread an aluminum sheet on a baking tray.
- Take chicken cubes in a bowl. Add ginger-garlic paste, salt and pepper powder and mix well. Set aside for 10 minutes.
- Combine cheese, green chilli and chopped coriander in another bowl and mix well. Add mace powder and nutmeg powder and mix again.
- Add egg and mix well. Add chicken and mix well. Add cream and mix well. Refrigerate to marinate for 2 hours.Skewer the marinated chicken cubes onto satay sticks, put the sticks on the tray, put the tray in the preheated oven and cook for 10 minutes, basting with butter at intervals.

- Serve hot.

Bhendi Anardana

Ingredients

- Ladyfingers (bhindi) slit 400 grams
- Pomegranate (anar) 2 tablespoons
- Oil 3 tablespoons
- Cumin seeds 1 teaspoon
- Green chilli chopped 2-3
- Small onions 12-15
- Red chilli powder ¼ teaspoon
- Turmeric powder ¼ teaspoon
- Coriander powder 1 teaspoon
- Dry mango powder (amchur) ½ teaspoon
- Salt to taste
- Garam masala ½ teaspoon
- Lemon juice ½ tablespoon

Method

- Put the anardana in a non-stick pan and dry roast lightly on low heat. Spread it on the tabletop and crush with a rolling pin.
- Heat sufficient oil in a non-stick kadai. Add cumin seeds and sauté lightly. Add green chillies and small onions and sauté till the onions become soft.
- Add ladyfingers and sauté for a while. Add red chilli powder, turmeric powder, coriander powder, dried mango powder and salt. Toss well.

- When the ladyfingers are almost done add the crushed anardana, garam masala powder and lemon juice and mix well. Serve hot.

Panch Ratan Dal

Ingredients

- ¼ Cup whole urad dal (black lentils)
- ¼ cup chana dal (Bengal gram split)
- ¼ cup moong (whole green grams)
- ¼ cup masoor dal (Egyptian lentils)
- ¼ cup tuar dal (Arhar/ pigeon peas)
- 2 small onions, finely chopped
- 1 tbspginger garlic paste (Garlic: optional)
- 2-3 green chillies
- 2 large tomatoes
- As per taste salt
- ½ tsp turmeric powder
- 1 tsp coriander powder
- 1 ½ tbspghee/oil
- 1 tsp cumin seeds A pinch of asafoetida powder (Hing)
- For garnishing coriander leaves

Method

- Mix, pick, rinse several times and soak the lentils in water for 1-2 hours.
- In a pressure cooker (or slow cooker) add the mix of lentils and pour some water, till the water level reaches above the level of lentils. Add salt and turmeric and pressure cook (or cook it, if using slow cooker) till 3-4

whistles of cooker.

- If cooking in a pan, let the water reach the boiling point and then simmer on low heat for 30 -40 minutes. Be sure to cover the pan and to stir the dal occasionally. Add some more water if needed.

- Meanwhile in a frying pan or kadahi, pour 1½ -2 tbspof ghee or oil and let it heat up. Carefully add a pinch of hing and some cumin seeds.

- When cumin is brown, add ginger garlic or just ginger paste, saute well, then add onions and sauté again till slight brown in colour.

- Add tomatoes, green chillies, coriander powder and cook well till oil separates out or till tomatoes are cooked well.

- Now just whisk the dal slightly and pour it in the pan or kadahi (you can pour the onion- tomato mixture in the cooker if your frying pan cannot accommodate the dal).

- Mix well, add some water if needed and cook on low flame for atleast 15 minutes or pressure cook it till 3 whistles of cooker. Simmer for 5 more minutes.

- Adjust the consistency of dal. This dal is supposed to be of creamy consistency. The longer you cook it on low flame, the more creamy texture is obtained.

- Garnish with coriander leaves.

- Serve it with rice/ roti.

Jeera Pulao

Ingredients

- 1 cup long grain Basmati Rice
- 2 cups Water + extra for soaking

- 1 tablespoon Ghee
- 1 Bayleaf
- 1 inch Cinnamon Stick
- 4–5 Cloves
- 1 teaspoon Jeera (Cumin Seeds)
- 1 Green Chilli,chopped finely
- ½ teaspoon Salt
- 2 tablespoons chopped Coriander for topping

Method

- Wash the basmati rice a few times, and then soak it in enough water so that the rice is completely soaked and has an inch of extra water on top. Soak the rice for at least 30 minutes.
- When you are ready to cook, drain all the water from the rice and set the rice aside.
- Heat ghee in a pot and add the whole spices and cumin seeds to it. Once the cumin seeds start spluttering, add the chopped green chilli and drained rice to it.
- Saute the rice in the pan for two minutes on a medium flame. This helps add more flavour to the rice.
- Add two cups water and salt to the rice and mix well.
- Bring the rice to a quick boil, and then reduce the heat to a simmer.
- Cover and cook for approximately five to six minutes, till all the water has evaporated and the rice is cooked through.
- Top with chopped coriander and serve hot.

Moong Dal Halwa

Ingredients

- ½ cup split yellow Moong dal, washed
- ½ cup unsalted butter (ghee)
- ½ cup sugar add 2 tablespoon more
- 1/8 tsp cardamom powder
- Few strands saffron
- 2 cups water For Garnishing
- 2 tbspsliced almonds

Method

- Wash dal thoroughly and soak in 3 cups of water for at least 4 hours. Drain the water and blend dal into a thick paste, adding just enough water as needed to blend.
- Boil water and sugar in a pan over medium heat, for 3-4 minutes. Remove from heat. Add cardamom powder and saffron; set aside.
- In a non-stick or heavy bottom frying pan add moong dal paste and melted butter. Mix well.
- Turn on the stove to medium heat and fully cook dal paste.
- Use spatula to gently press the paste, then fold the paste over and press again. Repeat this pressing and folding of the dal paste several times until the texture becomes grainy and light brown in color. This will take approximately 15 minutes, and will have a sweet, mild aroma when it is cooked.
- Lower the heat to medium-low. Add syrup to the dal, little at a time. The syrup will splatter as you are adding. Cover and cook for an additional 2-3 minutes.
- Remove cover, stir and cook for another minute.
- Turn off the heat. Garnish with almonds.

CHAPTER FOUR

Haryana – The Jat Land

"The name Haryana means the abode of God. It is a blend of two Sanskrit words 'Hari' which means God and 'Ayana' meaning home. Some say that the name has come from a compound of the words Hari (green) and Aranya (forest). It is a land where guests are treated equal to god."

Haryana has a rich cultural heritage that gives visitors the feel of the Vedic period. The state has its own rich customs and traditions, as well as folklores to up-lift its great cultural heritage not just in India but in the whole world. The state enjoys a blend of urban and rural population and boasts a rich culture and tradition. If we talk about Haryana's cuisine, it evokes simplicity, having very common life style and a general daily routine.

Haryanvi cuisine is just like the people in Haryana - simple, grounded and inevitably linked to the land. You will not find people opting excessively for restaurant food, especially in the smaller towns, as home-made meals are most cherished, using ingredients grown mostly in their own land. Imagine a state in India where how wealthy an individual is judged by the number of cattle the individual has! Where the golden rays of the rising sun penetrate the verdant fields and the chirping of birds lend a sweet music to the ears. The hookas, the cows, the khaats, the milk, the paddy fields, the colorful festivals.....Yes, it is Incredible Haryana, also known as the —The Home of Gods‖. Haryana represents the face of modern India. The one which is heralding the future yet prides itself of being rooted in its magnificent culture. Today Haryana is positioned among one of the wealthiest and most economically developed regions in South Asia

GEOGRAPHY:

Haryana one of the north Indian states situated on the gigantic plains of Yamuna River was carved out of East Punjab long on 1 November 1966 on linguistic as well as on cultural basis, is one of the 29 states in India with Chandigarh is the capital. Haryana became one of the most economically developed regions in India with its agricultural bloom. The total area of the state is 44212 sq km. This state shares its border with Punjab, Uttar Pradesh, Rajasthan, Delhi and Himachal Pradesh. Most of Haryana is in the plains with the Aravali mountain range starting its westward journey from here. The Yamuna is the only major river that passes through this small state, which is one of the greenest in the country. There is a very good network of canals throughout the state, giving it the much-needed impetus for agriculture, the mainstay of Haryana‘s economy. Haryana has four main geographical features:

- Shivalik Hills to the north east- These hills are the source of the rivers like Saraswati, Ghaggar, Tangri and Markanda. Parts of Panchkula, Ambala and Yamunanagar districts.
- Ghaggar Yamuna Plain forming the largest part of the state which is highly fertile- Divided in 2 parts- the higher one is called Bangar and the lower Khadar.
- Semi- desert sandy plain in the south west- This area includes the districts of Sirsa and parts of Hissar, Mahendergarh, Fatehbad, Bhiwani and shares border with Rajasthan.
- Aravalli hills in the south- This is a dry irregular hilly area.

BRIEF HISTORY:

The Vedas, the most ancient manuscripts of the Vedic religion, stem from the area that is now known as Haryana. These Sanskrit documents were written by the Aryans, who descended into the region from the north between 2000 and 1500 BCE. Haryana is also considered to be the birthplace of Hinduism, which began to take discernible shape by the 2nd century BCE and had developed two distinct branches by the 4th century CE. The battle of Mahabharat fought between the Pandavas and the Kauravas in ancient texts, was fought in this state on a battlefield known as Kurukshetra. The boundaries of Kurukshetra correspond roughly to the state of Haryana. Thus according to the Taittiriya Aranyaka the Kurukshetra region is south of Turghna (Srughna/Sugh in Sirhind, Punjab), north of Khandava (Delhi and Mewat region), east of Maru (desert) and west of Parin. Various Puranas, specially Vamana

Purana, were composed in Haryana at various tirathas on the banks of Sarasvati River. Other major vedic era religious sites in Haryana are Adi Badri, Dhosi Hill and Kapal Mochan. The Vedic state of Brahmavarta is claimed to be located in south Haryana, where the initial Vedic scriptures were composed after the great floods some 10,000 years ago. Among the world's oldest and largest ancient civilizations, the Indus Valley Civilization sites at Rakhigarhi village in Hisar district and Bhirrana in Fatehabad district are 9,000 years old.

Lying across the route of overland incursion into India, Haryana has experienced many waves of migration over the millennia; a notable invasion was led by Alexander the Great in 326 BCE. The area also has been the site of numerous decisive battles of Indian history. Among the most significant of these conflicts were the Battles of Panipat, which occurred in 1526, when the Mughal leader Bābur defeated Ibrāhīm Lodīand established Mughal rule in India; in 1556, when Afghan forces were defeated by the army of the Mughal emperor Akbar; and in 1761, when Aḥmad Shah ʿAbdāli decisively defeated the Marathas, paving the way for British control in India. Also important was the Battle of Karnal, in 1739, when Nāder Shah of Persia dealt a blow to the crumbling Mughal Empire.

The area included in the present state of Haryana was ceded to the British East India Company in 1803. In 1832 it was transferred to the then North-Western Provinces of British India, and in 1858 Haryana became a part of Punjab. The union between Haryana and Punjab was awkward, however, largely because of religious and linguistic differences between the two regions: Punjabi-speaking Sikhs of Punjab vis-à-vis Hindi- speaking Hindus of

Haryana. By the first decades of the 20th century, agitation for a separate state of Haryana was well under way, led most notably by Lala Lajpat Rai and Asaf Ali, both prominent figures in the Indian national movement, as well as by Neki Ram Sharma, who headed a committee to cultivate the concept of an autonomous state.

Haryana remained part of Punjab after the partition of India and Indian independence in 1947, but the demand for separate states—supported by both Hindus and Sikhs—continued, undiminished. Indeed, the movement gained momentum, reaching its fullest intensity in the early 1960s. Finally, with the passage of the Punjab Reorganization Act (and in accordance with the earlier recommendations of the States Reorganization Commission), Haryana was separated from Punjab in 1966 to become the 17th state of India.

CULTURE AND TRADITIONS:

Dating back to 4,500 years the people of the Harappan civilization were the first to occupy the land of Harayana. Later the Aryans from Central Asia started to migrate from there and started settling down in places like Punjab and Haryana because of the mighty river and its tributaries in this area of the Indian subcontinent. Thus the current populations of the people Haryana has their ethnic origin to the Aryan race and are popularly known as Jat. This is clearly proved by the external features of the people who are tall with sharp features and wheatish colour. Though they are quite aggressive in nature they are very good at heart. The culture of Haryana dates back to the Vedic times and the people are noted for their rich cultural heritage. The people of Haryana are known for their rich folklore and strictly adhere to their own traditions and customs and follow meditation, Yoga and chanting of Vedic Mantras which has become an integral part of their life. This way of life of the people of Haryana is age old customs. The culture of the people is extoled by their seasonal and religious festivals. The people are known for their diverse races, cultures and faiths which are blended in the right proportion to become something truly India. Even today they are preserving and follow their old religious and social traditions including fairs and festivals which are celebrated following all the traditional customs.

Most of the people of Haryana have more or less equal social status. Elders are always respected highly irrespective of caste. They have a unique tradition regarding khaat (type of bed consist of wood and rope). They have different khaat for each member in the family and the head of the family or any other respectful person always sits along the head portion of the khaat. This is called respect in Haryana. Khat and hukka represent the values of Haryana. Small village problem is taken care by the committee of five members panch in panchayat of the village, headed by sarpanch, where as several panchayats are headed by a single "khap panchayat".

When it comes to marriage, a boy and a girl of the same gotra are not allowed to marry and the marriage is a must within the same community. If marriages do not take place within the same Jat then it is considered as a great disgrace to the boy or the girl family and is never accepted. Marriage within the same village is also not permitted even if the boy and girl qualify for marriage according to gotra restriction. By following this custom the people are able to maintain racial purity and this factor of limiting within the community helps in promoting good health and prevention of physical degeneration. The people of Haryana do not promote karewa or widow marriage which is a very big obligation among the community.

The costumes of the people of Haryana are very simple and contribute a lot to their culture. The status of the family is judged by their costumes. Men usually dress up themselves with dhoti, shirt, turban and a pair of shoes. The style of the turban varies for a Jat, an Ahir, a Rajput, a Bania or a Brahman. They are always found being wrapped by a blanket or chaddar. Costumes vary for the women folk especially for those of different communities. A Jat woman's costume consists of a ghaggri (a long skirt), shirt and a printed orhni which has long cloth used to drape the front area of her body. The Ahir women are characterized by their lehenga or petticoat tight blouse and orhni which are usually red or yellow in colour and decorated with bosses and fringes. The costume of a Rajput woman is very much similar to that of an Ahir woman where the only difference lies in her orhni which is plain white with silver fringe but without a fall. The Brahmans and Aggarwal women go in for the normal dhotis and saris.

Irrespective of the community the people of Haryana in general have a lot of affinity for ornaments which are usually made of gold and silver. Some of their common or the most preferred ornaments include necklace, heavy bangles made of silver, jhalra (long hanging string of gold mohars or silver rupees) Karanphul and bujni of gold and dandle of silver for the ears. The rings which they wear on their fingers usually have their favorites name embedded in it. They also prefer nose rings and anklets.

The dance of the people of Haryana forms the basis of their art and infact it is also most commonly referred by the people as mother of all arts. Apart from dance, the delighting form of arts enjoyed by the people is Saangs, dramas, ballads and songs. They consider dance to be a way of expressing their physical and emotional energy rather just as a part of recreation for they believe that dance is a source of taking away the worries and stress of the performers. Punjab has influenced the people of Haryana a lot for the fact that culture and humour is very much similar to them. With Hindi as the base the people of Haryana speak numerous dialects.

CLIMATE:

Climate of Haryana The climate of the state is subtropical, semi-arid to sub-humid, continental and monsoon type. The summers are hot with maximum temperature of 48 Degree Celsius. Winds called 'Loo' blows during the month of May and June. The average rainfall of the state is 560 mm of which About 80% of the rainfall occurs in the monsoon season during the months of July and September. Winters are very cold and foggy, with temperature dips down to 3 Degree Celsius at some of the northern areas.

AGRICULTURE AND STAPLE FOOD:

Despite recent industrial development, Haryana is primarily an agricultural state and main occupation of the people of Haryana where they are involved in the cultivation of rice, wheat, jowar, bajra, maize, barley, pulses, sugarcane, cotton, oil seeds and potato. About 70% of residents are engaged in agriculture. The state owes a significant contribution in the GDP of India. Fertile lands, committed, hardworking and simple people. Haryana is at second position in food grain production in the country.

Haryana contributed significantly to the Green Revolution in India in the 1970s that made the country self-sufficient in food production. The world famous basmati rice is from Haryana. Nearly 70 % of the total population of people living here are into farming.

Dairy farming is also an essential part of the rural economy. Haryana has a livestock population of 98.97 lakh. Milk and milk products form an essential part of the local diet. Almost every household rear cows and buffaloes and are engaged in milk production. There is the saying "Desaan main des Haryana, jit doodh dahi ka khaana", which means "Among places is Haryana, where the staple food is milk and yoghurt ". The Murrah breed of water buffalo and Haryanavi cow from Haryana is world-famous for its milk production.

By the change of animal era to machinery period, Jats too have changes over to tractors and tillers in place of bullocks and jeep instead of horse. However a Jat in a village or on his farm cannot do without one or two buffaloes because without milk, curd, Ghee (clarified butter) and Chaach (cream separated curd), his daily diet remains incomplete.

CHARACTERISTICS AND SALIENT FEATURES OF THE CUISINE:

Haryanvi cuisine is like the people of Haryana - simple, earthy and inextricably linked to the land. There is no dearth of dairy products as it is one of the richest places in cattle population. Haryanvis believe in consuming the purest form of milk by petting cows and buffaloes at homes. People here make their own butter and ghee. Homemade fresh butter is called nooni or tindi ghee and is churned daily in most homes.

Jats are mostly non-meat eaters as a result of Vedic and Buddhist influences. Obviously the cuisine of Haryana has lot of dairy products and more of vegetarians. Their staple food is wheat or bajra, vegetables and plenty of milk and ghee. Jats consider non- vegetarian food undesirable but some of Jats started taking non- vegetarian food after German war.

Presently the proportion of meat eater Jats is very limited. Jat women are normally quite ignorant about cooking of non- vegetarian dishes. Jats earlier were not in habit of taking wine but it is slowly growing in modern times due to influence of other societies. Rice and Roti are most commonly eaten by the people of Haryana. The rotis are usually made either with wheat, barley, and gram flour. Some special varieties of rotis made in this region include Besan Masala Roti, and Bajra Aloo Roti. Gochini atta made from wheat and gram flour which is equally nourishing.

Curd, lassi, buttermilk, and sherbet are part of everyday Haryana food. Side dishes made of channa, cottage cheese, and spices commonly known as Kadai hara cholia is a very popular side dish for rotis. Steamed rice is served with Kadhi which is made with gram flour, onion, potato, curd, and spices along with aloo ke tikiyas. Parathas are eaten with a dish called bathua raita made with bathua, curd, and spices. Kichri, the porridge made from bajra, moong dal, or rice, is a nutritious evening meal of the rural people consumed with kadhi and pickle.

On special occasions halwa (ate ka halwa, gajar halwa, mongdal halwa, kheer and rabdi are prepared. Rice is consumed with a lot of ghee and sugar. Dal, churma, baati, lapsi, Gulgule and shakarpara are also very common. Papad and mangori are made from moong and moth which are used for vegetables throughout the year. Jat habitations have a plenty of kair and khejri trees. The fruit of kair is used as vegetable and in making curry. Kair is used in pickles and used throughout the year. Khejri pods, called Saangri in local language, are used as vegetables.

The 'Land of Rotis' is an apt title for Haryana, as people are fond of eating different kinds of rotis here. Wheat rotis are common and so are baajre ki roti and besan rotis, poories and chapatis. In earlier times, rotis would be made from a flour of wheat, gram and barley, a truly nutritious and healthy combination. Then there is the gochini atta made from wheat and gram flour. However with the rising price of gram and barley, people prefer the comparatively cheaper wheat flour, a loss both in terms of taste and nutrients.

Lassi made from yoghurt is another popular drink, almost a meal in itself. The Haryanvi's love for lassi can be gauged from the fact that thandai, a sweet, milk based drink is called kachi lassi.

SPECIALTIES DURING FESTIVALS AND OTHER OCCASIONS:

Kachri Ki Sabzi - is one of the most popular foods in Haryana. Kachri is a commonly found vegetable in the state. It is a wild variety of cucumber that resembles a small brown-coloured lemon. It is mostly consumed as a chutney or even sabzi, made with potatoes and other vegetables mixed together. The chutney has all sorts of ingredients including garlic, onion, aniseed (saunf), turmeric, cumin seeds, red chilies and salt to taste. It can stay fresh up to a month's time if refrigerated and kept properly in an air tight container.

Singri Ki Sabzi or Kair Sangri Ki Sabzi - which is mostly associated with Rajasthan, is also popular in Haryana. They are desert beans and berries that are used to make a lip-smacking stir-fry in Haryana. They are prepared by first soaking them in turmeric infused water overnight or boiling them with a dash of salt for about 15 minutes. Then goes the blend of numerous spices including dry mango powder (amchur), turmeric, chilli powder, coriander powder, garam masala, ground mustard, sugar and salt during the cooking process. You can add yogurt to it too. This sabzi can be enjoyed for a longer period once stored in the refrigerator, which is about 8-10 days, and can be savoured with dal ke parathe.

Hara Dhania Cholia- is chickpea or green chana which is commonly found in Northern India. Hari Dhania Cholia is a mix of green chana and variety of vegetables. It is prepared with onion, tomato, red chili powder, cumin seeds, coriander leaves and turmeric. It is a rare and unique combination that is popular in Haryana and is eaten with rotis or paranthas.

Methi Gajar- is a dish that most Indians are familiar with. This is a spicy preparation with little sweetness added to it with the help of carrots. Some people add a tad bit of sugar to maintain the balance. It's a popular dish in Haryana.

Kadhi Pakora- yogurt, coriander leaves, besan flour, green chillies, Mustard ghee, and cumin seeds along with curry leaves are the ingredients that result in delicious kadhi. Deep fried besan pakoras dipped in the khadi makes the dish irresistible.

Mixed Dal- Mixed Dal is a staple diet in Haryana. It is basically a blend of four to five protein-rich dals including chana, toor, masoorand moong. Prepared in pure desi ghee, it is mostly eaten with jeera rice. It also makes a delectable accompaniment for paranthas. It makes a distinctive staple with tomatoes, curd, garam masala and ginger garlic paste among others.

Rajma Chawal- This delicious Rajma sabzi is served with hot steaming rice. Rajma is very good for health as it is a high-protein source for the vegetarians. The food of Haryana is lip-smacking and different in its own way. Whether it's the sweet dishes, the several types of rotis or mixed dal, it's going to make you fall in love with its authentic taste.

Kaddu ki subji- Pumpkin is gourd like squash in yellow and round shape. Pumpkin curry or Kaddu ki sabzi is very easy and simple to prepare, chop the pumpkin and cook with spices and with chapatti and poori.

Bajra Khichri- Since bajra is one grain that is found in abundance in Haryana, making khichdi out of it seems quite an obvious thing to do. The delicious concoction of ground spices, some juicy vegetables and the hard crop makes for a delicious and heavy meal.

Bathua Raita- Bathua Raita is a yogurt recipe that is very refreshing and gives added benefits to health. Bathua or chenopodium leaves are anti oxidants and are rich in many vitamins. To prepare this dish, ingredients like chopped bathua, cumin powder, red chili powder and salt are added to the yogurt. Raita can be served along with almost all meals in Haryana.

TamatarChutney- Tamatar (tomato) chutney is spicy, tangy chutney made from tomatoes, onion, garlic, spices, salt and a pinch of sugar. The chutney can be served with pakoras or just on the side with any meal.

Kachri Ki Chutney- This lip-smacking chutney is prepared from a locally grown fruit/vegetable called

Kachri. The vegetable looks a lot like parwal and is a wild variety of cucumber. Mixed with garlic, onion, yoghurt and other spices, the ground concoction is mighty delicious

Besan Masala Roti-Makhan- is made with gram flour (besan), whole wheat flour (atta), gheeand the masala. The masala generally consists of cumin powder, coriander powder, dry mango powder (amchur), red chili powder, green chili paste and salt.

Bajra Aloo Roti-Makhan- It is prepared with a mix of bajra flour, mashed potatoes, ginger garlic paste, coriander leaves, garam masala. It served hot with white butter and it tastes heavenly.

Bhura Roti-Ghee- rotis dipped in ghee and eaten with bhura (powdered jaggary or sugar. The leftover rotis with these combination is extremely yummy.

Alsi ki Pinni- Pinni is an immensely popular sweet in Punjab, but Alsi Ki Pinni from Haryana is a different ball game altogether. It is prepared with alsi (lin seed or flaxseeds), whole wheat flour, sugar, ghee, nuts and cardamom powder. This sweet is not only amazingly delicious but also very healthy. Alsi is high in fiber, omega 3, iron and potassium among others.

Mithe Chawal- is prepared with rice, sugar, and ghee. To add color you can even use small quantity of saffron and cardamom. This mouthwatering dish will really add a taste for the whole day.

Churma- a simple but heavenly dish of roti, sugar and ghee which Haryanvi wrestlers have as part of daily diet and credit their strength to – does not offer it on the same plate but separately as a full breakfast dish or as an after-meal sweet dish.

Malpua or pua- the sweet fried pancakes served along with their sweet syrup or rabdi.

FESTIVITIES:

The state of Haryana celebrates the rich, glorious culture of India in its various fairs and festivals that are celebrated with equal pomp and gaiety here as all over the country. There are several fairs and festivals in Haryana that attract a large number of visitors to the state at different times of the year. These festivals are occasions of celebration, fun and frolic when the entire state of Haryana bustles with life.

Kurukshetra Festival – The festival in Kurushetra occurs in the month of November/December and coincides with the Gita Jayanti, signifying the birth of the Srimad Bhagavad Gita, the holy book of the Hindus. A visit to Kurukshetra during the festival is an exhilarating and spiritual experience. The pilgrims all gather to take a holy dip in the Brahma Sarovar and the Sannehit Sarovar, the waters of which are considered sacred. Week -long Bhagwad katha (presenting stories in Bhagwad Gita, sacred book of the Hindus), Shloka recital, bhajan, dance, dramas and 'deep daan' at Brahma Sarovar are part of the religious festivities.

Mahabharata Festival –This most popular festival is held every year in the month of December, at Kurukshetra, to commemorate epic battle of the Mahabharata. Though the time for celebrating the Mahabharata Festival almost coincides with the celebrations for the Gita festival at the same place, the Mahabharata Festival in Haryana takes place on a much larger scale and has wider participation. It is celebrated with a number of events and celebrations which include recitation of the Shrimad Bhagwad Gita, whereby homage is paid to the Epic Mahabharata and Lord

Krishna. A number of seminars and interesting discussions upon Bhagwat Gita is held which empanels different scholars and specialists from across the globe.

Baisakhi at Pinjore – Baisakhi festival in Pinjore, a small town in Haryana, is a grand event that is celebrated with much pomp and gaiety among the locals as well as visitors from across the country. It is celebrated to mark the start of the wheat harvest season. The festival falls on 13th April every year and is also observed as the first day of the New Year as per the traditional Vikrami calendar in India. Baisakhi at Pinjore is an equally frolicsome occasion when people adorn themselves with the best of apparels and jewelry, visit temples and gurudwaras to offer prayers and feast with loved ones. Another popular feature of the festival of Baisakhi in Pinjore is the performance of folk dances by men and women on dhol beats that is a must-watch. Mock duels, Bhangra and Gidda performances make the procession more joyous and colourful.

Teej – Teej heralds the onset of Sawan (monsoon), which is necessary for the agricultural prosperity of the state. Dressed in all their finery, with mehndi on their hands, the womenfolk converge to welcome the rains. The festive occasion has them on their feet with gidda and kikli (two folk dances). Makeshift swings are hung from trees and the women frolic on them, singing the traditional bojeeyan and tappe. Songs are also sung in praise of Goddess Parvati, as it was on this auspicious day that Parvati, the consort of Lord Shiva, won him after much penance. This festival too, is celebrated in both Punjab and Haryana. The festival is held at number of places in the state. Women accessories like bangles, mehndi and other makeup utilities are displayed here along with local handicrafts.

Holi and Deewali – These Hindu festivals are observed with great zeal and enthusiasm in every part of the state.

Lohri– This is an important Haryana festival for the farmer community. It marks the end of winter and welcomes spring- vasant ritu which is also known the season of fertility and love. It is celebrated on 13th or 14th January as per the lunar Indian calendar. It is celebrated one day before Makar Sankranti (Makar Sankranti Marks the transition of the Sun into Makara rashi (Capricorn). The legend which is associated with Lohri is the legend of Dulla Bhatti. In the evening we used to make a huge bon fire and used to sing the songs of Dulla Bhatti around it. We also used to throw popcorns, mishri (crystallised sugar), chuare (dried dates), puffed rice into the burning flame. Makki di rotl, sarson da saag, gajak and Gajar halwa are fovourite dishes served.

Haryana Day – Haryana Day is a regional public holiday observed on 1 November to celebrate marks the formation of the state of Haryana. The festival is held with great pomp and gaiety. This day also marks the Pakwan Pratiyogita (cookery completion), Run for Fun event, blood donation camps and various competitions along with musical performances in the evenings that are held almost in all tourist complexes in Haryana. All the state complexes and buildings are brightly lit up and decorated and present a cheerful and beautiful sight.

Pinjore Heritage Festival – It is organized to promote the rich cultural and historical tradition of the region and to celebrate the erstwhile heritage of the town of Pinjore. Dancers, theatre troupes, artisans and many more creative practitioners set to embellish the sprawling Pinjore Gardens. Festival is mainly an exhibition of the culture and tradition of the state. As a cultural concoction, this affair is attended by artists from all over the country who showcase their art and contribute towards the success of the event. It is one of the best places for the local artisan to showcase their creativity in handicrafts.

Gangaur festival – This festival is all about honouring Goddess Gauri or Parvati, and celebrating marriage and love falls on the onset of Holi and lasts for 18 days. Processions are taken out on this day with the idol of the Goddesses which is blissful for everyone. A lot of rituals are religious songs are performed in the temples on this day. People offer sweet dishes to the Goddess and pray for wealth and prosperity. In this fiesta, both married and unmarried women take part in full enthusiasm. Gana signifies Lord Shiva, and Gangaur symbolises Lord Shiva and Parvati together. As per legends, Gauri won Lord Shiva's affection and love with her deep devotion and meditation. And after that, Gauri visited her paternal home during Gaugaur to bless her friends with marital bliss. Gangaur festival is altogether a very colourful affair, which attracts a huge number of tourists.

Baisakhi – Baisakhi festival in Haryana is celebrated to mark the start of the wheat harvest season. The festival falls on 13th April every year and is also observed as the first day of the New Year as per the traditional Vikrami calendar in India. Baisakhi is celebrated to welcome the harvesting of wheat, so it is a Thanksgiving Day. After taking an early bath in ponds or rivers people visit temples or Gurdwaras to express gratitude to the Almighty for the bountiful harvest and pray for prosperity and good times in future. This day also marks the anniversary of the founding of "Khalsa Panth" among the Sikh community. High point of Baisakhi celebrations in villages is the performance of traditional folk dance bhangra and gidda by men and women respectively. The dance is simple in movement but is extremely energetic and is performed in-groups on the beat of dhol.

Gugga Naumi – This is a seven day long religious festival, celebrated all over Haryana in August-September paying respect to snakes and Gugga Pir or Zahir Pir (the saint) who is reputed to have the power to curing snake bites. He is also referred to as Beggar wala because of his grave near Dadrewa near Ganga nagar, a tract over which he is said to have ruled. The devotees worship the idol of Gugga Pir which they called „Gugga Kichhari". The temple is covered with colorful flowers, flags and other paraphernalia and the devotees sing folk songs which talked about the miracles performed by the great devine. Sevian (sweet vermicelli) is served to the guests as prasad.

Surajkund – The festival's name Surajkund derives its name from ancient amphitheatre resembling Greek amphitheatre constructed in 10th century AD by Raja Suraj Pal, one of Tomar chieftains in Faridabad. This is unique monument was built to worship Sun God (Surya). This is one of the largest crafts fair in India which has spectacular showcase of regional and international crafts, handlooms, traditions along with some mouth-watering multi-cuisine food for the visitors. The place is setup as a typical rural marketplace displaying the rich arts and traditions of India by the skilled artisans, sculptors, weavers and craftsmen. To give the fair a complete traditional touch, traditional cultural programs are held and rural cuisine is served. The fair is truly the most popular among all fairs and festivals in Haryana and attracts visitors in large numbers from all parts of the country. Surajkund Crafts Mela is an annual confluence of India's culture and folk traditions that is organized on a large scale by Haryana Tourism from 1st to 15th February.

Kartik Fair– The Kartik Cultural Festival is held at the Nahar Singh Mahal in Ballabgarh town organized by Haryana Tourism working with Ballabgarh Beautification Society and a number of allied agencies. The main aim of this festival is to promote the fort ambience, martial arts, Indian classical music and dance and a rich variety of folk theatre. The festival had given new life to dying folk arts, martial arts and worked to bring traditional folk dances and music to the national stage.

Somwati Amawasya – This fair is held twice a year in the month of May and October in the name of pitra-tarpan on the bank of Sohana river, where as per the Hindu calendar Shraadh is observed to bring peace to the dead souls of the ancestors. While the men are busy with the rituals, the women cook a special dish with wheat and jaggery near the river on wood fire which is served to the departed souls (shraddh arpan). People take dip in the Sohana river hoping to get relief from the sorrows and prosperous future. Women tie thread around papal tree trunk, chanting slokas or singing local folksongs. The festival is accompanied by large fair where artisan sells their products like shawls, bangles, jewellary, toys etc. Food stall sprayed around serve intra as well as interstate cuisines.

Mango Festival – It is observed to popularize and enhance and highlight the tremendous popularity of the mangoes. During this festival many different varieties of mangoes from all over India are showcased. Competitions held between mango growers from all over the country and the visitors get the chance to taste all the different and traditional varieties of these summer fruit. Apart from mangoes, latest hybrid fruits from the different agricultural universities are also exhibited. Fruit products like jam, pickles and canned fruits from various agro industry and food companies are also displayed. Various kinds of cultural programs and functions take place. The Mango Festival in total also reflects the enriching cultural extravaganza of Haryana.

Recipes from the Haryanvi Cuisine:

Kair Sangri Ki Sabzi

Ingredients

- ¾ cup Sangri
- 2 tablespoons Ker
- 2 Dry red chillies , broken into pieces
- ½ teaspoon Ajwain (Carom seeds)
- ¼teaspoon Asafoetida (hing)
- ½ teaspoon Turmeric powder (Haldi)
- 1-½ teaspoons Red chilli powder
- 1 teaspoon Amchur (Dry Mango Powder)
- 2 teaspoons Coriander Powder (Dhania)
- 1 tablespoon Jaggery , optional
- ¼cup Raisins
- 4 sprig Coriander (Dhania) Leaves
- Cooking oil , for cooking

Method

- To begin making the Ker Sangri Sabzi Recipe, soak the ker and sangri immersed in lot of water for at least 8 hours or overnight.

- After 8 hours, drain the water and rinse the ker sangri in water a couple of more times, to remove residual dust and dirt.
- In the next step, we will cook the soaked ker sangri in the pressure cooker. Place the soaked Ker Sangri in the pressure cooker, add 1 cup of water and cook the ker sangri until you hear 3 to 4 whistles.
- After 3 to 4 whistles, turn off the heat and allow the pressure to release naturally.
- The next step is to combine it with spices and make the Ker Sangri Sabzi
- Heat a tablespoon of oil in a heavy bottomed pan over medium heat. Add the ajwain, the red chillies and allow it to roast a little. Add the cooked raisins, the turmeric powder, asafoetida powder, coriander, amchur powder and finally the Ker Sangri and give all the Ingredients a good stir.
- Stir fry until all the Ingredients are combined and allow it to cook for another 5 minutes. Once done, turn off the heat and the Ker Sangri Sabzi is ready to be served.
- Serve the Ker Sangri Sabzi along with Kadhi, Phulkas and Steamed Rice and not to forget the ghee along with.

Besan Masalas Roti

Ingredients

- 1 cup besan (gram flour)
- 1 cup atta (whole wheat flour)
- ½ tsp turmeric powder
- 1 teaspoon ajwain (caraway or carom seeds)

- 1 teaspoon salt
- ½ cup curd | yogurt (optional)
- Water to knead
- For the Masala filling
- ½ tsp red chilli powder
- ½ tsp cumin powder
- ½ tsp coriander powder
- 1 TbspGhee

Method

- Add the flour, salt, ajwain and turmeric powder in a mixing bowl. Mix well. Add the curd, and then sprinkle water little by little to form slightly firm dough. Rest it for about 20 minutes.
- Mix all the Ingredients mentioned under masala filling and keep aside.
- Take the rested dough and divide into 8 portions. Take a portion and flatten it slightly. Dust some flour on the rolling surface (minimum flour as needed) and some on top of the dough. Roll it out into a small disc (approx 3 cm).
- Brush the surface with ghee and sprinkle the masala filling evenly. Then you can fold this into a triangle or a circle.

For triangle:

- Fold it into half. Fold again from one side to another to for a triangle. Now roll the folded triangle as thin as possible.
- Start rolling the disc into a cylinder with the stuffed masala inside.

- Heat the griddle | tawa on medium heat. Once it is hot, place this on the tawa. In 10-15 sec flip it. Apply some ghee on top and then again flip it and apply ghee on other side. Now cook both sides until brown spots appear and it may slightly puff.
- Follow the same procedure with the remaining dough.
- Serve it immediately with a spicy side or a simple yogurt.

Mixed Dal

Ingredients

- 1 cup chana dal
- 1 teaspoon turmeric
- 1 small onion
- 1 clove garlic
- 1 teaspoon cumin seeds 2 tablespoon butter
- handful coriander leaves
- ½ cup urad dal
- 1 ½ teaspoon salt
- 1 small tomato
- 1 green chilli
- 1 red chilli
- 8 ml vegetable oil
- 1 teaspoon red chilli powder

Method

- To make this delicious recipe, soak the chana dal and urad dal separately for about 15 minutes. Wash them twice or thrice and keep separately.

- Take a pressure cooker and fill it with 2 cups of water and chana dal. Add salt and turmeric powder. Cook until 2 whistles and turn off the gas. Let it cool.
- Add soaked urad dal into the boiled chana dal, cook until 2 whistles. Keep the cooker aside.
- Now take a non-stick pan and heat oil and butter on a medium flame. Then add 1 tbspchopped garlic and ginger. When garlic becomes a light brown in colour, add chopped green chilli, cumin seeds along with whole red chillies and saute for 3-4 minutes.
- Add chopped onion in the pan and saute until the onion becomes translucent. Now add chopped tomato into it. Cook until the tomato becomes tender or soft. Add red chilli powder, saute it and turn off the gas. Pour this tempering on the dal and the mix dal is ready. Garnish dal with chopped coriander leaves and serve hot with roti, rice or naan.

Bhura Roti Ghee

Ingredients

- 3 home made rotis or 3 wholewheat tortillas (see tips)
- 2 ½ tablespoons ghee
- 3 tablespoons goor (jaggery or palm sugar – see tips), plus more if you like it sweeter
- 3 tablespoons ground almonds
- couple of strands of saffron
- a large pinch of ground ginger

Method

- Reheat the rotis or whole-wheat tortillas, if using, in a toaster oven for a minute on the lowest setting. Or heat on a hot griddle for a minute each, turning over half way. Tear into small pieces and place in a large shallow bowl.
- Scatter on the ground almonds and dot with goor or palm sugar, if using.
- Heat the ghee over medium high heat till hot but not burning hot. Gently drizzle over the mountain of roti, goor and almonds. There is something therapeutic about this, so take your time. Crumble the saffron in your palm and sprinkle over the mixture. Dust on the ground ginger and, with not so nimble fingers, gently knead the Ingredients so that they meld into each other. This is an act of love so try not to be in a rush.
- The mixture should be warm. If it has cooled a bit, simply toss into a frying pan and heat gently. Tumble the ghee, goor and roti into a bowl and serve immediately.
- Ghee, goor and roti can be doled out into bowl and eaten with a spoon.

Malpua

Ingredients
For malpua

- 1 cup maida / plain flour / all purpose flour
- ½ cup rava / semolina / bombay rava / sooji
- ¼ cup sugar
- ½ tsp fennel / saunf, powdered
- ¼ tsp cardamom powder / elachi powder
- ½ cup milk / rabri
- water as required, to prepare batter

- oil for deep frying
- rabri for serving
- dry fruits for garnishing

For sugar syrup:

- 1 cup sugar
- ½ cup water
- ¼ tsp cardamom powder / elachi powder
- few threads saffron

Method

- Firstly, in a large mixing bowl take maida, rava and sugar.
- Also add fennel powder and cardamom powder.
- Further add milk or rabri.
- Mix well making sure there are no lumps in the batter.
- Add water as required and mix well.
- Make sure the batter is of smooth poring consistency.
- Further whisk the batter for atleast 5 minutes.
- Cover and rest the batter for 30 minutes.
- Pour the batter into hot oil / ghee.
- Once the malpua starts to float, splash oil over malpuas.
- And also press gently with the help of perforated spoon.
- The malpuas will puff up like poori.
- Now fry both sides till they turn golden brown.
- Drain the malpuas onto the a kitchen towel to remove excess oil
- Now soak the malpuas into hot sugar syrup.
- Rest for 10 minutes making sure both the sides of malpua are soaked well.

- Finally, serve malpuas hot with rabri and garnished with few nuts.

Kachri Ki Sabzi

Ingredient

- 1 cup Gawar Phali (Kothavarangai / Cluster beans), chopped
- 9 Kachri (Wild cucumber) , chopped
- 1 tablespoon Cooking oil
- 1 tablespoon Cumin seeds (Jeera)
- 1 teaspoon Asafoetida (hing)
- 1 tablespoon Turmeric powder (Haldi)
- 1 tablespoon Red chilli powder
- Salt , to taste
- ¾ tablespoon Coriander Powder (Dhania)
- 1 tablespoon Amchur (Dry Mango Powder)

Method

- To begin making Rajasthani Kachri Phali Ki Sabzi Recipe (Wild Cucumber And Beans Sabzi), peel and cut wild cucumber, make sure you taste them before adding with other Ingredients as sometimes they can be bitter in taste.
- Take a pressure cooker. Add gawar phali and pressure cook them for one whistle and release pressure immediately.
- Take a strainer and strain water and keep them aside.
- Heat oil in a pan or kadai on a medium heat, add cumin and asafetida once the oil is hot.

- Let cumin crackle and add turmeric powder, red chilli powder, and coriander powder. Mix everything well for few seconds.
- Add chopped kachri and mix it with masala. Let it cook for about 5-7 minutes.
- Now add boiled gawar phali to cooked kachri. Let it cook for about 2 minutes on medium heat. Add salt to taste and amchoor powder.
- Serve Kachri Phali Ki Sabzi Recipe (Wild Cucumber And Beans Sabzi) along with Phulka, and Smoked Dal Makhani Dhaba Style Recipe for a weekday lunch.

Hara Dhania Cholia

Ingredients

- Green Bengal Gram 3 cups
- Yogurt to taste
- Oil 3 tablespoons
- Onion 1 large
- Asafoetida ¼teaspoon
- Cumin seeds ½ teaspoon
- Green chillies 2-3
- Garlic paste ½ tablespoon
- Ginger paste 1 tablespoon
- Turmeric powder ¼teaspoon
- Coriander powder ½ tablespoon
- Cumin powder 1 teaspoon
- Red chilli powder 1 teaspoon
- Yogurt 1 ½ cup
- Garam masala powder 1 teaspoon

Method

- In a pressure cooker cook hara cholia with 3 cups of water half teaspoon salt for 20-25 minutes (2-3 whistles).2. Drain all the water and keep it aside. Now, heat oil in a deep non-stick pan.
- To this add asafoetida and cumin seeds to the pan. Sauté these till the seeds splutter.
- Now, add onion to the pan and saute for 1 minute. Now, add green chillies, garlic- ginger paste and sauté till fragrant.
- Add turmeric powder, coriander powder, cumin powder and red chilli powder and mix well. And close the lid and cook for few munites. Now, add yogurt, cholia and salt to taste and mix well.
- Add ¼ cup water and garam masala powder and mix. Cover and cook for 3-4 minutes. Serve hot.

Rajma Masala

Ingredients
For pressure cooking:

- 1 cup rajma
- 1 bay leaf
- 1 black cardamom
- 1 tsp salt
- 4 cup water

Other Ingredients:

- 1 tbspghee / clarified butter

- 1 tsp cumin / jeera
- 1 inch cinnamon
- 5 cloves
- 1 onion, finely chopped
- 1 tsp ginger garlic paste
- 1 chilli, slit
- 2 cup tomato pulp
- ¼ tsp turmeric
- 1 tsp kashmiri red chilli powder
- 1 tsp coriander powder
- ½ tsp cumin powder
- ½ tsp aamchur / dry mango powder
- ½ tsp garam masala
- ½ tsp salt
- 1 tsp kasuri methi, crushed
- 2 tbspcoriander, finely chopped

Method

- In a large kadai heat 1 tbspghee and saute 1 tsp cumin, 1 inch cinnamon and 5 cloves. Add in 1 onion, 1 tsp ginger garlic paste, 1 chilli and saute until the onions turn golden brown.
- Now add 2 cup tomato pulp.
- Cover and cook for 10 minutes, or until the oil is separated.
- Further keeping the flame on low add ¼ tsp turmeric, 1 tsp chilli powder, 1 tsp coriander powder, ½ tsp cumin powder, ½ tsp aamchur, ½ tsp garam masala and ½ tsp salt.
- Saute until the spices turn aromatic.
- Add in cooked rajma and mix well.

- Cover and simmer for 15 minutes or until the curry thickens.
- Now add 1 tsp kasuri methi, 2 tbspcoriander and mix well.
- Serve hot.

Besan Masala Roti

Ingredients

- 1 cup besan (gram flour)
- 1 cup atta (whole wheat flour)
- ½ tsp turmeric powder
- 1 teaspoon ajwain (caraway or carom seeds)
- 1 teaspoon salt
- ½ cup curd | yogurt (optional)
- Water to knead
- For the Masala filling
- ½ tsp red chilli powder
- ½ tsp cumin powder
- ½ tsp coriander powder
- 1 TbspGhee

Method

- Add the flour, salt, ajwain and turmeric powder in a mixing bowl. Mix well. Add the curd, and then sprinkle water little by little to form a slightly firm dough. Rest it for about 20 minutes.
- Mix all the Ingredients mentioned under masala filling and keep aside.

- Take the rested dough and divide into 8 portions. Take a portion and flatten it slightly. Dust some flour on the rolling surface (minimum flour as needed) and some on top of the dough. Roll it out into a small disc (approx 3 cm).
- Brush the surface with ghee and sprinkle the masala filling evenly. Then you can fold this into a triangle or a circle.
- For triangle:
- Fold it into half. Fold again from one side to another to for a triangle. Refer the stepwise pic. Now roll the folded triangle as thin as possible.
- Start rolling the disc into a cylinder with the stuffed masala inside.
- Heat the griddle | tawa on medium heat. Once it is hot, place this on the tawa. In 10-15 sec flip it. Apply some ghee on top and then again flip it and apply ghee on other side. Now cook both sides until brown spots appear and it may slightly puff.
- Follow the same procedure with the remaining dough. Serve it immediately with a spicy side or a simple yogurt.

Alsi ki Pinni

Ingredients

- Alsi 500g (flax seeds or linseeds)
- Wheat flour 500g
- Ghee 400g
- Sugar 750g
- Almonds 100g

- Raisins 100g
- Pistachios 100g
- Cashew nuts 100g
- Green cardamom powder 1,tsp (heaped)
- Gond 100g (gum arabic)

Method

- Heat a pan and roast the alsi on medium flame till fluffs up and place it in a plate.
- In a pan heat ghee 200g and roast the wheat flour, till light golden on a medium flame, once roasted keep aside in a plate.
- Heat ghee 100g and fry the gond till it fluffs up on a medium flame, and keep aside.
- Now grind the roasted alsi (flax seeds) keep aside, and grind the gond and keep aside as well.
- Cut the nuts and keep aside.
- Now heat ghee 100g in a pan ad roast the alsi (flax seed) for 5 minutes on a low to medium flame, and then keep aside.
- Make the sugar syrup add sugar in a pan with 2 cups 0f water and cook it till you make a 1 thread consistency.
- Now in a large pan add the wheat flour, gond, nuts, green cardamom powder, alsi mix well and then add the sugar syrup.
- You have to work fast or the sugar will dry in the mix, so take hand full of the mix and squeeze and make round balls, can grease your palms if required.
- Keep in air tight boxes.

CHAPTER FIVE

Uttar Pradesh and Bihar - The Real Deal

Known for its royal cuisine with delectable flavours, Awadhi cuisine has a specific style of cooking that brings out the real essence of the delicacies. Lucknow, the capital of U.P extends along banks of the river "Gomthi". The creator of Lucknow as it is today is Nawab Asaf ud Daula. After the battle of Buxar, the rulers of Awadh, turned their attention to more peaceful pursuits. The city became known as the centre of Urdu poetry and country diction, and reached its' acme during the reign of Wajid Ali Shah, who was a connoisseur of food. During this time the bawarchis (cooks) of Awadh were the ones who first brought the concept of the 'dum' style of cooking or the art of cooking over a slow fire. It is this combination of slow cooking with perfect ingredients that brings the flavours‖. Lucknow is known for its elaborate cuisine, 'chikankaari' (embroidery on muslin cloth) and the 'Pehle Aap' tradition (emotional warmth and high degree of hospitality). The culinary skills were raised to a fine art under the royal patronage, a favourite pastime of Nawabs of Awadh being perfecting the art of cooking. Although Awadh is not a state, the Mughlai food of Lucknow is commonly known as Awadhi cuisine. In the times of the nawabs this region was known as Awadh. Awadh region constitutes the area of Lucknow, Kanpur, Allhahbad and Varanasi in U.P. Lucknow, commonly known as the 'city of nawabs', reflects the Persian culture of art, curtly manners, poetry, and fine cuisine. The Awadhi cuisine is greatly influenced by Mughal cooking techniques, it bears similarities to the cuisines of Persia, Kashmir and Hyderabad.

The dishes of Bihari cuisine are consumed not just in Bihar but in Jharkhand and Eastern Uttar Pradesh too. It includes Bhojpuri, Maithili and Magahi cuisine. The characteristic feature of Bihari cuisine is the predominant use of mustard oil along with a tadka (tempering) of panch phoran literally the "five spices" including cumin seeds (jeera), fennel seeds (saunf), fenugreek seeds (methi), mustard seeds (sarson) and nigella seed (kalonji or mangrael). Bihari cuisine involves a lot of light frying (bhoonja). Another feature is the use of smoked red chilli in mustard oil to bring flavor and aroma to the food.

Regional Geography:

Theoretically and historically what came to be the Mughal suba of Awadh (in the United Provinces), with its capital as Ayodhya, stretching from Ganga to the Gandak, entirely consisting of alluvial plains. By and large it corresponded to the 15th century Sharqi kingdom with its capital at Jaunpur on the Gomti and to the ancient Kosala, with its earlier capital at Sravasti and later at Ayodhya. With the changing period its boundaries were changed, rivers were the links to the different states, later Awadh region was roughly described as the country between Ghaghara and Gomati west to the line from Ayodhya to Sultanpur, this division included present district of Faizabad, some portion of Lucknow, Sitapur, Barabanki and north of Sultanpur). To the east and west it is enclosed by the older acquired districts of the North West provinces – with Jaunpur, Basti, Azamgarh on one side and Sahajahanpur, Farrukhabad and Kanpur on the other. Awadh is situated, a little westward of the centre of that portion of the Gangetic plain. In nutshell Awadh is bounded by the Ganges Doab to the southwest, Rohilkhand to the northwest, Nepal to the north, and Purvanchal to the east. Its inhabitants are referred to as Awadhis. The major rivers of Awadh are the Yamuna, Ganges, Ghaghara and Sarayu.

Brief History:

Awadh's political unity can be traced back to the ancient Hindu kingdom of Kosala, with Ayodhya as its capital. It was taken by Muslim invaders in the 12th century and became part of the Mughal Empire in the 16th century with Faizabad as its initial capital and Saadat Ali Khan as its first Subadar Nawab and progenitor of a dynasty of Nawabs of Awadh (often styled Nawab Wazir al – Mamalik). British interest in Awadh began in the 1760s, and after 1800 they exercised increasing control there. It was annexed (as Oudh) by the British in 1856, an action that greatly angered Indians and which has been cited as a cause of the Indian Mutiny (1857–58), the largest Indian rebellion against British rule. Lucknow, the region's most populous city, was the scene of much fighting during the unsuccessful revolt. In 1877 the British – controlled Oudh region was joined with Agra to form the United Provinces of Agra and Oudh. The traditional capital of Awadh was Faizabad, but the capital was later moved to Lucknow, also the station of the British Resident, which now is the capital of Awadh. After India's independence in 1947 that territory became part of Awadh.

Culture and Traditions:

The culture of the people of Awadh is very much fascinating and captivating. The people are known for their rich cultural heritage where they adhere to their traditional customs and practices. Apart from its natural gifts the people have nurtured a rich heritage of cultural elements. The people of Awadh take the pride of bestowing the two great epics in Indian history namely Mahabharata and Ramayan.The culture of Awadh , thus, has rightly imbibed this trend and manifested it in its various features. It is highly essential to mention about the fairs and festivals celebrated by the people which gives a glory to the culture of the people. Apart from the national festivals like Holi, Diwali and Makar Sankranti which are celebrated with great fervor the people also fete on many regional festivals and fairs like Taj Mahaotsav which attracts people from all over the globe. This festival recalls the inheritance of the Mughal era by displaying the fine marble replica toys of the Taj, Mughal jewelry, 'zari' clothing and much more. The festival of Kumbhmela is celebrated with following of religious practices and traditional customs. During the months of October – November the Ganga festival is celebrated on the banks of the river Ganga and the same is worshipped. The other major celebrations of festivals and fairs include Lucknow festival and Bateshwar fair. Most of the festivals here are accompanied by events like kite flying, chariot race, and pigeon flying which are memories of the Hindustan Nawabs and is an integral part of the festival.

The people of Awadh follow the ritual or more than that they make it compulsion in one's life time of taking a dip in the holy water of river Ganga and Yamuna. They believe that by having a bath in this holy water they get purified from all the sins they have committed in their life time. Aarti is another important ritual which is followed in the Ganga ghats. The deities are offered with light from the wicks soaked in purified butter in a very grand manner. Havan is a ritual performed by the people of Hindu community. It involves lightning of holy fire or the Yagna and the belief is that by doing this all evils and ill – wills are thrown apart. It is considered very auspicious among the Hindus to perform a Havan for the prosperity and the good luck before starting of any new work. This puja is conducted by the chief priest and during which lots of mantras are recited. They follow the patriarchical system of society or social structure.There is a great harmonical balance between all sects and religion. Awadh is the most populated state in the country with 175 million inhabitants, out of whom 81% follow the Hinduism, 18% follow the Islam, and the rest belongs to the religion of Sikhism, Jainism, Buddhism and Christianity. In the Hindu community there are various sub groups based on the caste they belong to. The Brahmin is the most superior caste followed by the Kshatriyas, Vaishayas, they dominate the economic and political sector over the centuries and are in minority. The schedule casts schedule tribes and the backward class forms the majority and lives in rural areas. *Ganga – Jamuni tehzeeb*, that poetic Awadhi phrase for a distinctive, syncretic Hindu – Muslim culture is also reflected in the many crafts and weaves — in their form, symbolism, aesthetics and spiritual connotations. For example Kashmiri Muslim carpet makers feature Durga in their patterns, Muslim sculptors making idols of Durga, and Hindu craftsmen create the Muharram tazia. Even though having too many religions and castes the people of the state has lived in complete tranquility.

Climate:

Purvanchal's climate can be referred as humid subtropical climate with dry winters. It experiences all the 4 seasons and commonly has a climate with humid temperature. Winter season falls from November till February where in some parts of the northern region the temperature dips to 0 degree centigrade. Thick mist and fog can be observed in the northern plains. It is followed by summers between March to June where the maximum temperature rises to 48 degree centigrade. The monsoon season falls between June and September. Variations in climate occur at different parts of Purvanchal. Many a times the region experiences single climatic pattern with minor variations due to the uniformity of the vast Indo – Gangetic Plain. Cyclical droughts and floods due to unpredictable rains are experienced in many parts of the state due to variations in climate. Rainfall in state can vary from an annual average of 170 cm in hilly areas, to 84 cm in Western parts of the state. Relative humidity is low, that is around 20 per cent and dust winds blow throughout the season.

Staple food:

Awadh is one of the major contributors to the national food grain stock and some of the major crops grown here include wheat, rice, maize, sugarcane, oilseeds, potatoes, cotton, tobacco, jute and pulses. Wheat and rice are the staple food of Awadh people. This is partly due to the fertile regions of the Indo – Gangetic plain and partly due to irrigation facilities such as canals and tube – wells. Pulses, wheat, rice, potatoes and oil seeds are the major agricultural products produced in the state. Sugarcane is the most important cash crop throughout the state. Lakhimpur Kheri is a densely populated sugar – producing district in the country. Awadh region shares 70% of the total sugar production in the country. Vegetables of all kind are well grown in this Indo – Gangetic plain. As far as horticulture is concerned, Awadh is an important state. Intensive plant cultivation is practiced all around the state. Apples, guava, litchi, water melon, musk melon and mangoes are highly produced. Due to extensive agricultural activity cattle farming is also well established. Buffaloes, cows and goat milk are abundantly available.

Special Characteristics:

Lucknow being the capital of most of the Nawabs, so the food culture of this place is widely developed and propagated. The region is famous for its Nafasat (Refinement) and Nazaakat (Delicateness), which can be seen in its kebabs and other Nawabi food which bears more or less similarities to Mughlai, Kashmiri and Hyderabadi cuisine. The secret of Awadhi cuisine lies in the manner in which the food is cooked on a slow fire and the spices used while making a dish. It does not use of hundred odd spices to produce each dish but a blend of handful uncommon spices. A whole battalion of chefs used to serve the nawabs of Lucknow. Each chef had his own secret recipe which he used to impress the nawab and gain favours. An Awadhi cuisineis majorly adorned by three kinds of cooks –

- Bawarchis – the experience cooks who cooked food for big gatherings in large quantities.
- Nanfus –nanfus made selection and preparation roti, chapattis, naans, sheermals, baquarkhani, kulchas and taftans.
- Rakhabdar – they used to cook in small quantities and responsible for garnish and presentation of the food.
- Daroga – e – Bawarchikhana(Head of kitchen)

Apart from these there were helpers who assisted the above in the preparations, like –

- Kanhaar – water boys
- Mehrin – utensil cleaners
- Masalchi – who grinds masalas

There were competitions organized for chefs to prove their talent. The best dish or the one most liked by nawab was then rewarded. Thus each chef tried to do his best and present the most exotic dish. The bawarchis (chefs) and rakabdars (gourmet cooks) of Awadh invented the dum style of cooking or the art of cooking over a slow fire which was unique because it not just retained the flavours and aroma of the food, but also the nutrients.The richness of Awadh cuisine lies not only in the variety of cuisine but also in the ingredients used like mutton, paneer, and rich spices, which include cardamom and saffron.

"Dastarkhwan, a Persian term, literally means a laid – out ceremonial dining spread. It is customary

in Awadh to sit around and share the Dastarkhwan. The Babarchis of Awadhi transformed the traditional dastarkhwan with elaborate dishes like kababs, kormas, kaliya, nahari – kulchas, zarda, sheermal, roomali rotis and parathas. There are also other important processes such as marinating meats in order to produce a delightful taste. Fish, red meats, vegetables and cottage cheese may be marinated in curd and spices. This helps to soften the taste and texture of them as well as remove any undesired odors from the fleshy materials.This is especially the case with barbecued food that might be cooked in a clay oven (tandoor) or over an open fire (sigri). Some of the tawa preparations are in fact equally, if not more famous like tandoori kebabs and tikkas."

The menu changes with the seasons and with the festival that marks the month. The severity of winters is fought with rich food. Paye (trotters) are cooked overnight over a slow fire and the shorba (thick gravy) eaten with naans. Turnips are also cooked overnight with meat koftas and kidneys served during lunch. This dish is called shab degh and is very popular in Lucknow. Birds like partridge (Teetar) and quail (Batair) are eaten from the advent of winter since they are heat giving meats. Fish is relished from the advent of winter till spring. Zarda Pulao is favourite during Spring season. In summers coolants likeAam ka panna, Shikanji and lassi are had as a part of a daily meal. Fruits such as mango, melons, water melons are also consumed in great quantities. Chutneys, Murrabbas and Achars are made in great quantities. Lots of Raitas are also eaten. It is avoided in the rainy season. In Awadh river fish are preferred particularly rahu (carp) and fish kababs (cooked in mustard oil) are preferred.

Green peas are the most sought after vegetable in Awadh. One can spot peas in nimona, salan, qeema, pulao or just fried plain. Spring (Sawan) is celebrated with pakwan (crisp snacks), phulkis (besan pakoras in salan), puri – kababs and birahis/berani (paratha stuffed with mashed dal) khandoi/dhoka (steamed balls of dal in a salan), laute paute(gram flour pancakes— rolled, sliced, and served in a salan), Patoda OR Seodha(colocasia – leaf cutlets served with salan) add variety. In summer, raw mangoes cooked in jaggery or sugar, make a dessert called galkaalso raw mangoes cooked with virmicilli or semolina, jaggery or sugar called shakramba. These dishes come from the rural Hindu population of Awadh.

Activity in the kitchen increases with the approach of festivals. During Ramzan, the month of fasting, the cooks and women of the house are busy throughout the day preparing the iftari (the meal eaten at the end of the day's fast), not only for the family but for friends and the poor. Id is celebrated with varieties of Siwaiyan (vermicelli). Muzzaffar is a favourite in Lucknow. Shab – e – barat is looked forward to for its halwas, particularly of semolina and gram flour. Khichra or haleem, a mixture of dals, wheat and meat, cooked together, is had during Muharram, since it signifies a sad state of mind.

Some dishes appear and disappear from the Lucknow Dastarkhwan seasonally, and others are a permanent feature, like qorma, chapatti, and roomali roti. The test of a good chapatti is that you should be able to see the sky through it. The dough should be very loose and is left in a lagan (deep broad vessel) filled with water for half an hour before the chapattis are made.

Sheermals were invented by Mamdoo bawarchi more than one and a half century ago. They are saffron covered parathas made from dough of flour mixed with milk and ghee and baked in iron tandoors. No other city produces sheermals like Lucknow does and the festive dastarkhwan is not complete without it.

Spices used in Awadh cuisine:

All Spice (Kebab Chini), Bay Leaf, Asafoetida or Hing, Liquorice, saffron (kesar), Black Peppercorn, Star Anise, mace (javitri), dried lemon grass (jarakush), sandalwood, rose petals, alum, vetiver, Cinnamon, Clove, Cardamoms i.e. Badi Elaichi, Chotti Elaichi, royal cumin (shahi jeera), Caraway Seeds (jeera), Coriander, Chilies and Fenugreek. A popular spice mix called Lazzat –e –taam is used to flavour dishes.

Kebab: Kebab's are the integral part of Awadhi. Lucknow is proud of its Kebabs. There are several varieties of popular kebabs in Awadhi cuisine viz. Kakori Kebabs, Galawat ke Kebabs, Shami Kebabs, Boti Kebabs, Patili – ke – Kebabs, Ghutwa Kebabs and Seekh Kebabs are among the known varieties. The kebabs of Awadhi cuisine are distinct from the kebabs of Punjab insofar as Awadhi kebabs are grilled on a chulha and sometimes in a skillet as opposed to grilled in a tandoor in Punjab. Awadhi kebabs are also called "chulha" kebabs whereas the kebabs of Punjab are called "tandoori" kebabs.The Seekh Kebab has long been considered a piece de resistance in the Awadhi dastarkhwan. Introduced by the Mughals it was originally prepared from beef mince on skewers and cooked on charcoal fire. Now lamb mince is preferred for its soft texture.The 100 – year – old Tunde ke Kabab in Chowk is the most famous outlet for Kababs even today. Tunde kabab is so named because it was the specialty of a one – armed chef. The tunde kabab claims to be unique because of the zealously guarded family secret recipe for the masala (homemade spices), prepared by women in the family. It is said to incorporate 160 spices.*Kakori kabab* is considered blessed since it was originally made in the place by the same name in the dargah of Hazrat Shah Abi Ahder Sahib with divine blessings. The mince for the kabab comes from the *raan ki machhli* (tendon of the leg of mutton) other ingredients include khoya, white pepperm and a mix of powdered spices that remains secret.*Shami Kebab* is made from mince meat, with usually with chopped onion, coriander, and green chillies added. The kebabs are round patties filled with spicy mix and tangy raw green mango. The best time to have them is May, when mangoes are young. When mangoes are not in season, kamrakh or karonda may be substituted for kairi, as both having a tart flavour reminiscent of the raw mango.A variant made without any mixture or binding agents and comprising just the minced meat and the spices is the *Galawat kabab.*An unusual offering is the *Pasanda Kebab*, piccata of lamb marinated and then sautéed on a griddle.*Boti kebab* is lamb marinated in yoghurt and skewered, then well cooked. Traditionally, Boti Kebab (Lamb) is cooked in a clay oven called a tandoor.Vegetarian kebabs include *Dalcha Kebab, Kathal ke Kebab, Arbi ke Kebab, Rajma Galoti Kebab* (kidney bean kebab cooked with aromatic herbs), *Zamikand ke Kebab* (Lucknowi yam kebabs), etc.

Curry preparations:

Korma is actually the Indian name for the technique of braising meat. It originated in the lavish Moghul cuisine wherein lamb or chicken was braised in velvety, spiced sauces, enriched with ground nuts, cream and butter. While kormas are rich, they are also mild, containing little or no cayenne or chillies.There are both vegetarian (navratan korma) and non – vegetarian (chicken, lamb, beef and fish korma) varieties of korma. Murgh Awadhi Korma is a classic from Lucknow. **Kaliya** is a mutton preparation with gravy along with the compulsory inclusion of turmeric or saffron.

Rice preparations:

Lucknowi biryani –

Biryani derives from the Persian word Birian, which means "roasted before cooking." Biryani is a mixture of basmati rice, meat, vegetables, yogurt, and spices. Lucknow biryani or awadh airyani is a form of pukki biryani. Pukki means "cooked." Both meat and rice are cooked separately, then layered and baked. The process also lives up to the name biryani in the Persian meaning "fry before cooking'.

It has three steps. First, the meat is seared in ghee and cooked in water with warm aromatic spices till tender. The meat broth is drained. Second, the rice is lightly fried in Ghee, and cooked in the meat broth from the previous step. Third, cooked meat and cooked rice are layered in a handi. Sweet flavours are added. The handi is sealed and cooked over low heat. The result is a perfectly cooked meat, rice, and a homogenous flavour of aromatic meat broth, aromatic spices and sweet flavours.

The vegetarian version of biryani might have some textured vegetable protein based protein balls to present the impression of a meat – based dish for vegetarians. The difference between biryani and pullao is that pullao is made by cooking the meat in ghee with warm aromatic spices until the meat is tender, then adding rice and cooking in the sealed pot over low heat till done—but with biryani, the rice is boiled or parboiled separately in spiced water and then layered with meat curry or marinade (depending on the type of biryani), then sealed and cooked over low heat until done.

Tehri – Tehri is the name given to the vegetarian version of the dish and is very popular in Indian homes.

Bread Preparations:

As wheat is the staple food of the state, breads are very significant. Breads are generally flat breads; only a few varieties are raised breads. Tawa roti is bread made on crude iron pans. Improvisations of the roti (or bread) are of different types and made in various ways and include the rumaali roti, tandoori roti, naan (baked in a tandoor), kulcha, lachha paratha, sheermaal and baqarkhani.

Breads made of other grains have descriptive names only, thus we have Makai ki roti, Jowar ki roti (barley flour roti), Bajre ki roti (bajra is a grain only grown in India), chawal – ki – Roti (roti of rice flour).

- Chapati is the most popular roti in India, eaten for breakfast, lunch, or dinner.
- Puri are small and deep fried so they puff up.
- Paratha is a common roti variant stuffed with fillings of vegetables, pulses, cottage cheese, and even mince meat and fried in ghee or clarified butter. This heavy and scrumptious round bread finds its way to the breakfast

tables of millions.

- Rumali Roti is an elaborately prepared ultra thin bread made on a large, convex metal pan from finely ground wheat flour. The Urdu word rumaali literally means a kerchief.
- Tandoori Roti is a relatively thick bread that ranges from elastic to crispy consistency, baked in a cylindrical earthen oven. The Urdu word tandoor means an oven.
- Naan is thick bread, softer and richer in texture and consistency than the tandoori roti. It is made from finely ground wheat flour kneaded into a very elastic mass.
- Sheermaal is a sweetened Naan made out of Maida (All – purpose flour), leavened with yeast, baked in a Tandoor or oven. It typically accompanies aromatic quorma (gravied chicken or mutton). Originally, it was made just like Roti. The warm water in the recipe for Roti was replaced with warm milk sweetened with sugar and flavoured with saffron. Today, restaurants make it like a Naan and the final product resembles Danish pastry.
- Baqarkhani is an elaborate variation of the sheer – maal that is fried on a griddle rather than baked in a tandoor.

Desserts:

Winters are dedicated to halwas of all kinds that came from Arabia and Persia to stay in India. There are several varieties of these, prepared from different cereals, such as gram flour, sooji, wheat, nuts and eggs. The special halwa or halwa sohan, which has four varieties, viz Papadi, Jauzi, Habshi and Dudhiya is prepared especially well in Lucknow.

The Jauzi Halwa Sohan is a hot favourite even today, but the art of preparing it is confined to only a few households. Prepared for the most part from germinated wheat, milk, sugar, saffron, nuts etc., it has love and patience as its vital ingredients.Ananas Ka Muzaffar – Electric yellow rice with sugar syrup, pineapple chunks and ghee. Shahi Tukra – Shahi means — Grand Tukra means — Pieces — Here the grand refers to the richness of the dish. Fried breads dip in sugar syrup simmer in balai / rabari. Tradionally cooked or served from Mahi Tawa.

Chaat:

Chaat and Samosa originated in Uttar Pradesh but now are popular nationwide and abroad. These are the integral part of street foods across India. The chaat variants are all based on fried dough, with various other ingredients. The original chaat is a mixture of potato pieces, gram or chickpeas and tangy – salty spices, with sour home – made Indian chilli and Saunth (dried ginger and tamarind sauce), fresh green coriander leaves and yogurt for garnish, but other popular variants included Aloo tikkis (garnished with onion, coriander, hot spices and a dash of curd), dahi puri, golgappa, dahi vada and papri chaat. masala dosa is originated here.

There are common elements among these variants including dahi, or yogurt; chopped onions and coriander; sev (small dried yellow salty noodles); and chaat masala, a spice mix typically consisting of amchoor (dried mango powder), cumin, Kala Namak (rock salt), coriander, dried ginger, salt, black pepper, and red pepper. The ingredients are combined and served on a small metal plate or a banana leaf, dried and formed into a bowl. Sherbat is a well – known beverage in Awadhi cuisine, and is served especially during the summers. It tends to be a mixture of simple lemonade and complex drink of milk with crushed almonds. It is always served cold, and may also be quite filling. One of my other favourite hot beverages to consume on the chilly evenings of winters in Lucknow is the Kashmiri teaor NoonChai, this amazingly pink beverage is made from the same tea leaves as green tea but varies dramatically in taste. A bit salty and incredibly creamy, this chai (tea) is as unique in taste as it is in appearance. Paan was frequently consumed by the Nawabs and their Begums. GiloriLucknowiPaan, was carefully crafted and modified to comply with the royal taste of Lucknow

Culinary Common Terms:

Baghar– A method of tempering a dish with spices in hot oil or ghee, when making any curry dish the tempering is done before the curry is made and when any dal preparation is made, tempering is done with the help of a ladle at last to give a finishing taste.

Dhungar/Dhunger– A smoke procedure to impart flavor to meat dishes, the smoke enhances the aroma of the food making the meat tender and delicious.

Dum Dena – Dum means breathe, the process is done by cooking in sealed large pot, which is cooked over slow charcoal fire. One of the famous dish cooked by this process is Biryani or Dum Pukht Biryani.The chefs of Awadh are credited with invention of Dum Pukht Biryani.

Gile Hikmat – means Covered with clay, generally used to prepares Kushtas (whole vegetable or meat stuffed with spices and nuts, covered with banana leaf and then clay, buried in the heat of oven.

Galavat/Galawat– The process of adding softening agents to meat in order to tenderize it. One such preparation is Galavati Kebab. Papain, Kalmi Shora (KNO3) is few softening agent which is used in this process.

Durust Karna – Adjusting of the seasonings, spices or tempering especially ghee when the dish is almost done. One such process is called *ghee durust karna*. This is important to remove the raw flavor of the ghee or oil and flavor it with kewra, cardamoms.

Ghee Durust Karna – This is the process of removing the raw flavor from the ghee or oil so that it is does not overpower the flavor and aroma of the dish. This is done by adding Kevra water and cardamom. The ghee is reduced after adding the kevra and cardamom and then stored after straining it for further use.

Chandi ka warq – silver leaves used to decorate and garnish dishes like Chandi kaliya, Moti pulao, ladoos, burfi etc.

Zamin doz – In this style of cooking, a hole is dug in the ground and the ingredients are placed and covered with mud, then a layer of burning charcoal. The cooking takes about six hours.

Loab – It is a term used to refer a final stage of cooking, when the oil used in the cooking rises at the surface and floats on the top giving a finished appearance to the dish. Roganjosh is one such preparation in which oil floats at the top after the dish is done.

Moin – Process of shortening dough by kneading it with flour with fat. This makes the final product crisp and flaky. This process is used to make parathas and pooris.

Ittr – The use of perfumes play an important role in Awadh cuisine they are used to enhance the aroma of the dish and make it delicate. Most commonly used are rose water, kewra water etc.

Dastarkhwan - Dastarkhwan,a Persian term, literally means a meticulously laid – out ceremonial dining spread which is very elaborate. Many delicacies of the Awadh such as Kebab, Biryani, Korma, Roomali Roti, Parathas, Nahari, Kuchchas, Firni, Shahi Tukra, etc. are part of Dastarkhwan. It is customary in the Awadh to sit around and share the Dastarkhwan.

Common Characteristics of Awadhi Cuisine:

- Awadhi cuisine is an amalgamation of Persian cooking style blended with Indian ingredients and taste.
- Saffron is used in generous quantities in this cuisine.
- Rice is more commonly used staple.
- Slow cooking process (Dum Pukht) was used to ensure proper infusion of the flavours.
- Tandoori products are a prominent feature of the cuisine.
- The handwritten account of the royal kitchens of the Babarchis reveal that very few spices like cumin, coriander, ginger, pepper, cinnamon, cloves, and fennel were used in cooking. So, continuing the tradition, these are the very common ingredients used in the Awadh cuisine even today.
- All dishes as mild to medium – hot cream and nut – based gravies, rice dishes with lots of nuts, dried fruits and rich creamy desserts.
- Extensive use of milk, cream and butter in various gravies and curries makes the dishes even more appetizing with foodies ending up licking their fingers.

Almonds, pistachios, walnut, dried apricots and plums, and raisins are used in plenty in the stuffings, gravies, desserts etc. These make the dishes more exotic as compared to other cuisines.

- Herbs like mint, coriander and dill etc. also find common use in this cuisine.
- The use of sugar and saffron with lemon juice was common almost for every dish, perhaps, to create the sweet and sour effect. These also reduce the heat of the saffron which was used in large quantity. Curd is also widely used.
- Food is traditionally cooked in Desi ghee, lard obtained from the melted down fatty tail of sheep, apricot oil, and oil from the seeds of grapes. It is common to colour ghee differently with saffron, spinach, and turmeric and is flavoured with rose water musk and other perfumes.
- Awadhi biriyanis are Pakki biriyanis, where all the ingredients are cooked separately and then they are layered.
- Water for use in the cuisine was traditionally perfumed with camphor, dried lemon grass (jarakush), rose petals, sour orange leaves, sweet orange leaves and fennel leaves. Now such practices are rarely found.
- Because of the dominance of Muslim and Hindus by religion, pork and beef are traditionally not a part of this cuisine and instead heavily consumed and used goat, fowls, sheep, and venison in addition to vegetarian – based dishes.
- Fish is widely used and is made odour – free by applying the paste of fresh lime leaves, cardamom, cloves, lemon juice, and salt, and was kept overnight and then cooked with great skill so as not to leave any bone behind. Similarly, games were slaughtered and treated for

cooking. Traditionally, sandalwood paste was applied on them to remove unpleasant odour. The games are commonly smoked and grilled and barbecued meat adorns the table. Birds and animal of prey are commonly stuffed with rice, dried fruit and eggs to make a wholesome food. This style of cooking is given a more sophisticated touch now.

- Since Persian language was adopted by the emperors as the official language, thus many of the Awadhi dishes bear names in these languages.

Common Utensils:

- **Bhagona** –Or the patili is generally of brass with a lid. It is used when a great deal of'bhunna' or saute is required. or even for boiling and simmering. It is also usedfor preparingYakhni or Salan, Korma or Kaliya.
- **Deg/Degchi** – This is a pear –shaped pot with a lid of either brass, copper or aluminium.The shape of this utensil is ideally suited for the 'dum' method and is usedfor cooking Pulao, Biryani, Nehari or Shab Deg.
- **Kadhai** – Kadhai is a deep, concave utensil made of brass, iron or aluminium and isused far deep frying paoris puri and the like.
- **Lagan** –Lagan is a Tradition round and shallow copper utensil with a slightly concavebottom. Used for cooking whole or big cuts of meat or poultry especially whenheat is applied from both the top and bottom.
- **Lohe ka tandoor** –Is typically an iron tandoor, distinct from the clay tandoor which is morecommon in Delhi. It is a dome – shaped iron oven covered with iron sheet,

usedfor cooking a variety of Breads like – Sheermal, Taftan, Bakarkhani etc.

- **Mahi tawa** –Mahi tawa is the Awadh version of the griddle shaped like a big round, flatbottomed tray with raised edges used for cooking kababs. Also used for disheswhere heat is applied from both ends when covered.
- **Seeni** – Seeni is a big thali (round tray) usually used as a lid for the lagan or mahi tawawhen heat is to be applied from the top. Live charcoal is placed on it and the heatis transmitted through it to the food. Thus the indirect heat has the desiredeffect of browning and cooking the ingredients. All the copper and brass utensilsare almost always used after *'kalai'* or tin plating the insides.
- **Khurpa** – iron spatula with woden handle used while working with Lagan and making Galawat kebab.

Festivals:

- Annanas Ka Muzzafar: It is saffron flavoured rice with sugar syrup, pineapple chunks and ghee topped with crunchy paneer and nuts.
- Badam Halwa: It is made during festivals, special occasions like a wedding or a new home. In this halwa, badam is soaked and ground into a coarse semolina style mixture. It is roasted in ghee and then cooked in a saffron milk to give it that rich taste.
- Badami Murgh: Chicken cooked elaborately in different masalas. A true Nawabi feast.
- Bakarhani: It is soft flaky bread which is seasoned with cardamom and also sweet on the palate. It is usually

cooked in a tandoor which helps to give a charred and smoky flavour to the bread.

- Basket Chaat: It is a special chaat It is a special chaat served in a basket made out of deep fried sliced up potatoes basket. The chaat is garnished with curd, dry fruits, chaat masala and pomegranate seeds. The decoration is so beautiful and colorful, that your mouth will turn watery just by looking at it.
- Boorani: Garlic flavoured raita.
- Dahi Batashe: It is considered as a street food. We could spot those normal golgappa at every other place in North India, but this is a special one of Lucknow. The golgappas are filled with dahi, sweet flavored chutney and garnished with special chaat masala. Just writing about it makes my mouth watery.
- Dahi ke kabab: It is a type of shallow fried kabab made from hung curd, paneer, flour and basic spices.
- Galaouti Kebab: The name itself reveals the secret of this delicacy. The grinded flesh of lamb or beef mixed with the variety of spices provides it a perfect taste. The fried kebabs melt down as soon as you keep it on your tongue, reviving all the taste buds in your mouth.
- Gosht Kalia: Kashmiri lamb stew with milk and kashmiri Garam Masala.
- Handi Chicken: The dish is prepared in small handis by cooking rice, spices and chicken on low flame for hours until cooked. The handi is served packed to the customers.
- Kadhai Murg: The dish is very common one among all the Awadhi delicacies. The curry is medium spicy and the pieces of the chicken is cooked with the curry on low flame in a kadhai. Every bit of the spice added to the curry flavors the chicken. The tenderness of the flesh

increases due to low flame cooking.

- Kakori Kebab: It is the softest kebabs in the world which —melt in your mouth". Named after toothless king or Nawab of Kakori (a small town in Lucknow district).
- Khichra: Khichra is porridge like dish made from various dals, lamb, broken wheat and rice. Served mainly during Muharram.
- Kulcha: Leavened bread baked in tandoor.
- Kulfi Faluda: It is the most favorite dessert of Lucknowites. It is the combination of saffron flavored kulfi which is the iced milk and dry fruits garnished with falooda. The pleasant aroma of aroma and scented faluda will refresh you. It completes your five- course meal perfectly.
- Makhmali Murg: The sauce of this delicacy is made of milk and cream which gives it a white color. The pieces of chicken are soaked into this creamy sauce. The flavor of the sauce is sweetish and fascinating. The creamier the sauce the better it tastes.
- Makkhan Malai: The Awadhi cuisine is not just famous for its vegetarian and non – vegetarian dishes, but also for its amazing desserts too. This is a special dessert made of churned milk flavored with saffron and cardamom. It is lighter than air and you will not even feel a thing in your mouth except refreshing flavor of saffron, cardamom and dry fruits.
- Malai Ki Gilori: As the name suggests, this dessert is made of malai with the stuffing of dry fruits and mawa. The flavor of cardamom is quite pleasant. The outer covering of malai is decorated with an edible silver coating which is also known as vark and pista.

- Malai kofta: It is a popular Indian vegetarian dish made of potato, paneer balls dunked in smooth, rich, creamy gravy. Malai translates to cream and kofta to fried balls. So malai kofta literally translates to koftas dunked in creamy sauce or gravy.There are various versions of making this dish. The recipe of malai kofta that is shared here is not mughalai malai kofta which is served in white gravy.
- Motiya Chilman Pulao: It is rice preparation made in a pressure cooker and topped up with soft and crispy paneer balls.
- Murgh Do Pyaaza: So spicy, so easy! Chicken loaded with masalas & absolutely mouth – watering. Serve with a tandoori roti topped with butter, and go straight to heaven.
- Murgh – E – Kalmi: Chicken marinated in yoghurt and spices – grill it, bake it or use a tandoor.
- Musallam: It consists of whole chicken or mutton leg or vegetable marinated in a ginger – garlic paste, stuffed with boiled eggs and seasoned with spices like saffron, cinnamon, cloves, poppy seeds, cardamom and chilli.
- Mutton Boti Kebab: Thoroughly marinated, mutton cubes are cooked and then grilled on a skewer.
- Mutton do pyaza: The specialty of this dish is that its sauce is prepared of onions. The content of onions in its sauce provides it a very different flavor. The spices added to its sauce increase the aroma and deliciousness of the dish.
- Mutton Korma: The dish is prepared by cooking mutton in the spicy gravy made out of dry fruits, yogurt, and cream. The mutton is cooked on a low flame so that the spices added to the curry add its flavors to it. The mutton becomes tender and juicy in taste. It is served

with paratha or rice and tastes delicious.

- Muzaffar: Kheer made of vermicilli, khoya, milk and dried nuts.
- Nargisi Kofta: it is a dry kofta served as a starter. An innovative way of using the boiled egg wrapped up with spiced potato. The whole dish is then crumb fried in a shallow pan.
- Navratan Korma: It is a vegetable korma with nuts, paneer cheese, and an adjustable list of vegetables. It is in a tomato – cream sauce as opposed to the usual yogurt based sauce. 'Navratan' means 'nine gems,' so choose nine of the vegetable, nuts, and paneer ingredients.
- Neza Kebab: Popularly known as 'Lucknowi chicken lollypops', this kebab is prepared using chicken drumsticks, which are further marinated in vinegar and a mélange of spices. The marinated chicken drumsticks are then brushed with a mixture of roasted gram flour, whisked eggs and heavy cream. They are cooked on sigri.
- Nihari Ghost: It's a dish made of spicy sauce and tender meat. The content of sauce of this dish is more with tender mutton soaked into it. The spicy sauce of this dish will blow your mind.
- Nimona: The curry of a dish is made out of grinded peas with pieces of potato soaked into it. Every single vegetarian who tries it for the first time loves it. It is usually served with boiled rice and both make a great combination.
- Paneer KundanKaliyan: Succulent slices of cottage cheese cooked in a yogurt based gravy with onions, tomatoes and traditional whole spices. This delicacy is finished off with hints of garam masala and dried rose petals that bring a subtle flavour to this dish. Best

enjoyed with Indian breads.

- Pasanday: This is a traditional recipe of marinated mutton cooked in a spicy curry made with yogurt, cream, tomatoes and various spices.
- Patili – ke kebab: These are cooked using a patila or round shaped brass utensil. It is prepared by cooking minced meat in ghee and a variety of spices over slow flame. This method allows the kebabs to get a subtle aroma of the spices and a soft texture that gives you a melt – in – mouth experience.
- Phirni: Thick kheer made of ground rice, milk, khoya and nuts and served best in shikoras (clay bowls)
- Reshmi Kebabs: Tender minced meat kebabs with cream, kewra and nuts. Shallow fried and served with chutneys.
- Roomali roti: Rumali roti also called Manda is a thin flatbread originating from the Indian subcontinent, popular in India and in Punjab, Pakistan. It is eaten with tandoori dishes. The word rumal means handkerchief in many north Indian languages, and the name rumali roti means handkerchief bread.
- Seek Kebabs: Kebabs have always been an important part of Awadhi cuisine. These are special kebabs made of lamb. The lamb is blended with different special spices and cooked on the charcoal which provides it the tenderness and juicy flavor. The aroma of these kebabs is mouthwatering.
- Shahi Tudka: The word shahi always means royal, and that's what this dish is. The dessert is made of bread as its base with the topping of rabri and dry fruits, flavored with saffron and cardamom. The deep fried bread at the base is soaked in cardamom flavored sugar syrup. The aroma and presentation of this delicacy are amazing.

- Shakramba: A delightful tangy Khaṭṭa – Mitha exotic dessert made of primarily mango, semolina and milk.
- Shami Kebab: This kebab exists both as vegetarian and non – vegetarian dish. The minced meat or paneer is blended with all the 'khadda masala' to give it an Awadhi twist. These are so common in Lucknow that now it is considered as street food.
- Sheer branj: This is a mouth watering Persian rice kheer with Saffron, Rosewater, Khowa(mawa) and topped with Almond and Pistachio.
- Sheermal: It is an Indian famous flatbread which is flavoured with saffron. It is very soft and fluffy flat bread, it can be eaten along with different kind's curries. It is considered as one of the rare delicacies from Hyderabad and Lucknow.
- Sultani Dal: Toor dal simmered with milk , cream, and yogurt to make it a rich dish for the emperors to consume during their daily feast. A tempering of ginger, garlic , green chili, and spices give it a strong flavor which lifts the whole dish up.
- Taftan: It is leavened flour bread made with milk, yoghurt, and eggs and baked in a clay oven. It often flavoured with saffron and a small amount of cardamom powder, and may be decorated with seeds such as poppy seeds.
- Taheri: It is a traditional mixed rice with assorted vegetables that are locally available. The slight variation in this rice preparation is by adding curd to the gravy in order to give it a more authentic Awadhi touch to the whole dish.
- Tunday Ke Kebabs: These are categorized under must try dish of Lucknow. Their ancestors had served the

Nawabs of Lucknow. Preparation of these kebabs is very special and secretive, which they had been following since many years. These kebabs will melt in your mouth leaving indelible the flavor of each and every spice.

- Wadhi Biryani: One of menu favorite, it is a dish consisting of rice cooked with meat, different spices, and dry fruits. It is cooked in a special way known as —dum‖. The dish is always served with dahi raita and green chutney which adds up its flavor. The garnishing of a dish is done in a very different way i.e. with sliced up fried onions.
- Warqi Paratha: It's a layered paratha which is usually served with curry based dishes. It makes the perfect combination with non – vegetarian curry.
- Zarda: This delicacy is very rarely known and available to people. The dessert is made with special basmati rice flavored with cardamom sugar syrup. The saffron color and taste of the dessert is quite refreshing and mesmerizing. It is garnished beautifully with chandi vark and dry fruits. It is a must try dish.

Occasions not to miss:

- Ganga Dussehra – Ganga Dussehra is mostly celebrated in this particular region. The festival approaches in the excruciating summers in the month of June every year. Dedicated to the holy river Ganga, which acts as the lifeline of the people in here, the festival is highly awaited and the people participate in the celebrations with an insane level of excitement which is a great sight to savor. The festival lasts for 10 days.

- Buddha Purnima – The festival gets celebrated in the rest of the country as well, but in Awadh it holds a special significance for the people. Awadh is one of the most populated states in the country and it has people from all the religions in abundance. The Buddhist community is one among them and they are known to celebrate the birth of their lord Gautam Buddhawith great enthusiasm. This day is the most auspicious day for them in all year.

- Makar Sankranti – Entire country celebrates Makar Sankranti, mostly in the second or third week of January. But the festivals takes an entirely different shape in Awadh. The festival gets celebrated here in the months of December/January and the people take their ritualistic bath in the holy river, Ganga. There are few other customs and traditions which get followed and that make the Makar Sankranti celebrations different from rest of the country.

- Barsana Holi– Lath Mar Holi is the most colorful and a prestigious festival in Barsana near Mathura not be missed in Awadh. The festival takes place just few days before actual Holi. This festival time is a great holiday option for visitors which captures attention from tourists and pilgrims from all over the world. During the Holi celebrations, Ladies are found hitting sticks (laths) at each man as the common custom during this fest.

- Janmashtami– Mathura, the birthplace of Lord Krishna celebrates and rejoices the festival of Janmashtami with great enthusiasm. The major festival celebrations take place at Dwarkadhish Temple.

- Ramlila – Ramlila is famous for the enactment of the story of Lord Rama, on the basis of the holy epic Ramcharitmanas (written by the great saint Tulsidas). In several places, it is linked with Vijayadashmi celebrations on the occasion of Dussehra in late September or early October and also with Ram Navami, the birthday of Lord Rama.

- Taj Mahotsava – This is a grand festival organised in Agra (along the river Yamuna) by UP Tourism to pay a tribute to the legendary craftsmen of Uttar Pradesh. The festival exhibits the arts, crafts, culture and cuisine of the Braj area.

- Ramazan – This festival falls in the ninth month of the Islamic calendar, which lasts 29 to 30 days. All through the month of Ramzan the devout Muslims keep strict fast. They take food only before sunrise —Sehri‖ and after the sunset "Iftar". During the whole day they do the regular work and worship as usual. The food taken in Iftar is called Iftari and special delicacies like fried cornflower, boiled grams and lentils, meat kebabs and sweet meats are taken. This festival is intended to teach Muslims about patience, spirituality, humility and submissiveness to God. Muslims fast for the sake of God and to offer more prayer than usual.

- Eid – ul – fitr – means the joy at the end of the days of fasting. This is the day following the appearance of the new moon. The Muslims put on their best clothes. The Eid prayers are said between the early morning and the noon prayers. Once the prayer is over they greet each other– Eid Mubarak! Children are given special money called "Eidee" by their parents for buying toys and balloons on this day. Special delicacies are prepared. They include "Seviyan", vermicelli's sweet preparation, "Sheer Korma, and other savoury dishes.

- Eid – ul – zuha – It is one of the grandest festivals of the Muslims and it is also called Bakrid. It falls on the 10th day of the Muslim month of Zil– Hijja. On this day a ram or a goat or a camel is sacrificed and distributed among the near and dear ones.

- Milad – ul – nabi – This festival commemorates the birthday of Hazrat Mohammad and it falls on the 12th day of Rabi – ul – Awwal month. Prophet Mohammad was born in 571 A.D on April12th, in Mecca in Arabia. On this day the Prophet's teachings are repeated, the Quran is read and religious discourses are arranged in the mosques. The Muslims invite their friends and relatives for a grand feast on this day.

- Shivratri– Maha Shivratri that literally means the 'Night of Lord Shiva' is a prominent Hindu festival celebrated with enormous zeal and enthusiasm in various parts of the country. The festival is generally celebrated on the month of Phalguna or Maagh (February or March) according to the Hindu Lunar Calendar. On this auspicious day, people in large numbers, throng to temples and offer prayers to please the Lord. It is also believed that the Lord Shiva and Goddess Parvati married on this day. Many people also observe a fast on this day and offer sweets, flowers, milk and bael leaves on Shiva Linga.

- Muharram – This is the Muslim festival of mourning. Muharram is observed in the first month of the Hijri year. The Shia community in particular celebrates this festival called "Majlis – e – Shoora" with great enthusiasm. They fast, offer prayers and recite the Quran and sing elegies in homage to the martyrs during the celebrations. On the final day, Tajias are taken out in grand processions, accompanied by brass brands and bagpipes playing sad tunes. The Tajias represent the mausoleum of Hazrat Imam Hussain. The processions terminate at Karbala where the Tajias are ceremoniously buried. Muharram is in fact a sort of ceremony for showing gratitude to the departed souls who fought so bravely for preserving their faith.

- Shab - i – barat – The Muslims on this particular day, the fourteenth day of Shaban, God registers the actions of all men and dispenses their fates according to their deeds. It is celebrated with illuminations, fireworks and crackers. People distribute food and sweets in the name of their deceased ancestors and offer flowers for their graves. The shias associate this night with the birth of their last Imam.

- Raksha Bandhan – is a festival that is celebrated on the full moon day in the month of Shravan according to the Hindu Lunar calendar. This day is observed as the day of siblings as on this day sisters and brothers come together to express their love for each other and also pray for their wellbeing. The sisters tie a knot of rakhi on the wrist of her brother, who promises to protect his sister from the evil. People also tie rakhi to their friends and other close ones to spread love and care to them.

Bihari Delights:

The dishes of Bihari cuisine are consumed not just in Bihar but in Jharkhand and Eastern Uttar Pradesh too. It includes Bhojpuri, Maithili and Magahi cuisine. The characteristic feature of Bihari cuisine is the predominant use of mustard oil along with a tadka (tempering) of panch phoran literally the "five spices" including cumin seeds (jeera), fennel seeds (saunf), fenugreek seeds (methi), mustard seeds (sarson) and nigella seed (kalonji or mangrael). Bihari cuisine involves a lot of light frying (bhoonja). Another feature is the use of smoked red chilli in mustard oil to bring flavor and aroma to the food.

The staple food of Bihar is wheat and rice. Rice is also mentioned in Abul Fazl's Ain-i-Akbari as the staple diet of Bihar. A typical Bihari meal usually consists of dal, bhaat (rice), phulka (roti), tarkari (sabzi) and achar (pickles). Some of the famous Bihari delicacies include:

- **Litti Chokha**: It is a dough ball made up of wheat flour, stuffed with a mixture of sattu (chickpea flour) with spices and roasted over cow dung cakes, wood or coal and tossed with ghee. Litti is eaten with chokha which is a blend of eggplant, potatoes and tomatoes mixed with spices.

- **Bihari Kebabs**: Meat is cut into slices, mixed with a lot of spices and cooked over coal on skewers. Cooked kebabs are tossed with ghee.

- **Sattu Paratha**: Roasted chickpea flour is stuffed in paratha and then fried in ghee.

- **Pitha**: Small sized dumplings made of rice flour, stuffed with chana dal(Bengal gram) paste and steamed. It is served with coriander chutney.

- **Ghugni**: Black gram is soaked overnight and cooked with onions, garlic and garam masala. It is served with fried choora.

- **Choora**: Beaten rice which is either baked or fried. It is served with Ghugni, curd, jaggery and with a spicy preparation of peas and onions.

- **Thekua**: The Bihari version of cookies, it is made with whole wheat and jaggery and is deep fried. In the sacred festival of chhath, it is made as Prasad.

- **Til-Laddu**: Makar Sankranti is a major festival in Bihar and a huge variety of gajaks and til laddus are made during this festival.

- **Sattu Drink**: Made with roasted gram powder, water, rock salt and roasted cumin, it is as tasty as it is healthy. On most occasions it is a breakfast on the go for busy people.

- **Gaja**: They look like *shaker-pare* and are an essential part of the wedding snacks that the bride carries to her in-laws place.

- **Mutton curry**: For non-vegetarian Biharis, mutton curry made in mustard oil and ghee is the ultimate way to celebrate a joy.

- **Malpua**: Unlike the regular malpua, the traditional Bihari malpua has bananas in it. But it is also made sans bananas with loads of khoya and paneer, dipped in cardamom sugar syrup.

- **Makhana-Kheer**: Made with makhane, it is one of the most sought after vrat dishes which is also served as a dessert.

- **Khaja**: A must have preparation during weddings, this layered sweet is a pure delight. A place called Silav is said to make the most delicious Khajas.

- **Kala Jamun**: Kala Jamun is a version of Gulab Jamun, which is darker in colour and is filled with saffron syrup.

- **Jhalmuri**: While Bengal may lay a claim on this savory, spicy desi trail-mix made with puffed rice, mustard oil, onion and green chillies, it is so popular in Bihar that evenings are almost unimaginable without it.

- **Balushahi**: One of the most popular Bihari sweets, Balushahi, fried in desi ghee is among the most exchanged sweets during festivities. Silk-city, Bhagalpur is famous for its melt-in-the mouth balushahi.

- **Anarsa**: Gaya district (yes, you got it right-the land of Buddha) is famous for this mithai which is basically khoya ball, dipped in rice batter, coated with sesame seeds and deep fried.

"The Famous Litti and Chokha: Litti and Chokha is a popular delicacy of Bihar. It is also consumed in Jharkhand, parts of Eastern Uttar Pradesh and Nepal. Litti is a dough ball made up of wheat flour. It is stuffed with a mixture of sattu (chickpea flour) with spices, onions, ginger, garlic, lime juice, carom seeds and herbs.

Sometimes, pickles are also mixed to add to the flavor. Traditionally, this dough ball was roasted over cow dung cakes, wood or coal and tossed with ghee. In recent times, however, people choose to fry it for the sake of convenience.

Litti is eaten with chokha which is a blend of eggplant, potatoes and tomatoes mixed with spices. It is not cooked like a regular sabzi. The vegetables are first roasted, mashed and mixed with finely chopped onions and spices.

It's believed that litti emerged in Magadha, which was an ancient kingdom in southern Bihar. For a long time, litti and chokha was also associated with the peasants as it does not require expensive ingredients and the sattu in it especially has cooling properties which kept them active throughout the day.

It has been said that during the 1857 Revolt, this meal was preferred because it could be easily baked, with minimal ingredients, was filling in nature and could last up to three days. It's said that Tantia Tope and Rani Lakshmi Bai made it their travel meal. With the coming of the Mughals, this dish underwent some changes. Litti began to be served with shorba (meat's gravy) and paya (curry made up of hoof of goat, sheep, cow with spices and herbs). In contemporary times, litti and chokha transcends class boundaries and is eaten by every strata of Bihari society."

<u>Recipes:</u>

<u>Kakori Kebab:</u>

Ingredients –

- Minced Lamb – 1 Kg
- Raw papaya paste – 100 gm
- Salt – 1 Teaspoon
- Yellow chili, powdered – 4
- Powdered white pepper – 5 gm
- Powdered cloves – 8
- Powdered blades mace – 2
- Grated nutmeg – 1/8 Teaspoon
- Powdered black cardamom – 4
- Powdered green cardamom – 6
- Powdered coriander seeds – 10 gm
- To Prepare Paste Form
- Coconut – 50 gm
- Poppy Seeds – 10 gm
- Shahi jeera – 5 gm

- Khoya – 200 gm
- Fried brown & crushed onion – 100 gm

To Prepare Fine Paste:

- Garlic – 10 Pod
- Ginger – 10 gm
- Other Ingredients
- Roasted gram flour – 200 gm
- Pure ghee – 100 gm
- For Garnishing
- Some onion rings
- Green chilies slit

Method –

- Mince the lamb meat till very smooth then add papaya paste, powdered yellow chilli, white pepper, cloves, mace, nutmeg, black cardamom, green cardamom, and cumin seeds. Mix these ingredients well.
- Now to give dhungar* to the mixture, put the meat mixture in a deep pan and keep live coal in a small bowl in the centre, pour two tbsps of ghee on coal and quickly cover the pan. Keep covered for half an hour.
- Mix the pre – prepared coconut – onion paste, ginger – garlic paste.
- Add this mixed paste to the smoked mince. Set aside for another half an hour.
- Then, after adding roasted gram flour to the meat mixture and blend well.
- Heat skewers slightly and grease and take a portion of the mince mixture and spread on skewers with slightly wet hand into the oblong roll around the skewers.

- Roast on kabab griller on live coal for a few minutes till they turn to a golden pink – brown.
- Once the kababs are done take out carefully from the rods with the help of the cloth.
- Plate them on serving the dish and garnish them with onion rings, slit green chillies and fresh coriander chutney and serve hot.

Dhungar– It's a quick procedure to flavour meat. The smoke permeates each ingredient of the dish and gives an aroma which enhances the dish taste and quality.

Paneer Kundan Kaliyan:

Ingredients

- Paneer – 500 gm
- Kashmiri Red Chilli – 5 gm
- Coriander seeds – 5 gm
- Onion – 200 gm
- Tomato – 100 gm
- Green cardamom – 5
- Cloves – 10
- Garam masala powder – 5 gm
- Ghee – 40 gm
- Cream – 50 ml
- Curd – 100 gm
- Dried rose petals – 5 gm
- Salt – to taste
- Coriander – to garnish

Method

- Cut cottage cheese or paneer in thin slices. Marinate these with turmeric and chilli powder. Shallow fry.
- Heat oil in a pan. Add Kashmiri red chillies, coriander seeds, cloves and cardamoms to hot oil and saute till they change colour slightly.
- Add chopped onions till they are translucent. Add chopped tomatoes and dried rose petals. Saute this mixture for a few minutes.
- Add yogurt and garam masala. Whisk continuously on low flame so that the yogurt does not curdle. Once done, add shallow fried cottage cheese slices. Season with salt and garnish with coriander leaves.

Murgh Awadhi Korma:

Ingredients

- Ghee – 1 tbsp
- Green cardamom – 5
- Cloves – 5
- Black cardamom – 2
- Cinnamon stick – 1
- Chopped ginger – 1 ½ tsp
- Chopped Garlic – 1 ½ tsp
- Red chili powder – 1 tsp
- Coriander powder – 1 tsp
- Kasoori Methi (dried fenugreek leaves) – 1 ½ tsp
- Garam masala – 1 ½ tsp
- Brown onion paste – 1 Cup
- Cashew nut paste – ½ Cup
- Chicken – 300 gm
- Salt – 1 Tbsp

- Chicken stock – 250 ml
- Curd – 1 Cup
- Cream – 1 Cup

Method

- Heat ghee in a frying pan and add green cardamom, cloves, black cardamom and cinnamon in it and sauté it properly. This will take 30 – 40 seconds.
- Then add some ginger and garlic and sauté it, once their fresh fragrance gone and cooked, add red chili powder, coriander powder, kasuri methi,garam masala and brown onion paste, cashew nut paste. Give it a mix and let it cook for some time.
- After a minute add chicken pieces, salt and chicken stock in it and cover it with a lid and cook it for 10 – 15 minutes.
- Finally, add some curd and cream to the chicken mixture and transfer this to the serving bowl.
- Garnish this with almonds and coriander leaves and serve hot murgh Awadhi korma with chapatti.

Sheermal:

Ingredients

- All purpose flour / maida – 1 cup.
- Caster sugar – 1 – 2 tbsp.
- Salt – pinch.
- Ghee – 1 tsp.
- Butter – 1 cube
- Yeast – 1 tsp.

- Milk – 1 cup.
- Saffron colour – 1 pinch.
- Poppy seeds – 1 tsp .
- Fennel seeds powder – ½ tsp.

Method

- Take a bowl, add all purpose flour, caster sugar, little salt, ghee, butter, yeast, milk and mix nicely to make a little soft dough.
- Cover bowl with polythene sheet and allow it to rest for 1 hr.
- Divide dough into 2 portions and dust some flour and roll into small chapati.
- Transfer into a baking tray and give shapes like as shown in video.
- In a bowl, add milk, little sugar, saffron colour and mix nicely, later give milk wash to already prepared sheermal.
- On top it sprinkle poppy seeds, fennel seeds powder and allow it to proof for 10 – 20 minutes.
- Transfer into oven and bake it at 200 degree centigrade for 3 – 4 minutes.
- Arrange in a serving plate and give a butter wash.

Keshari Phirni:

Ingredients

- Rice flour – 30 gm
- Sugar – 60 gm
- Milk – 300 ml

- Pista – 10 gm
- Almonds – 10 gm
- Cardamom – 2 nos
- Silver foil – 4 sheets
- Khoya – 50 gm

Method

- Mix the rice flour with little cold milk and boil the remaining milk and add it to the prepared mixture.
- Cook slowly on a slow flame till it becomes slightly thick, add grated khoya.
- Draw out the pan to the side of the fire and sprinkle the sugar, mix thoroughly till the sugar dissolves.
- Add powdered cardamom.
- Pour in individual moulds, sprinkle chopped/sliced almonds and pista.
- Chill and decorate with edible silver foil.

CHAPTER SIX

Bengal – The Golden Fertile Land

Bengal has been famous for its food and cuisine ever since the establishment of civilization in the landscape made up of the sovereign state of Bangladesh (earlier East Bengal or East Pakistan) and the Indian state of West Bengal. Bengali cuisine generally involves a hot palette, using a large number of herbs, spices and roots in order to create dishes that are full of depth. However, these flavors can also be altered to create more delicate tastes, and it is important to note that dishes vary from region to region. The areas of West Bengal and Bangladesh are interesting for both their similar qualities, and inherent differences. Today, Bengal is divided between West Bengal and Bangladesh. This has been the case since the partition of Bengal which took place in 1947, and led to some small but important changes in both areas.

"*The city of Kolkata within West Bengal became a multicultural hub and thriving port, whereas Dhaka within Bangladesh was in a way disconnected from this, and independently maintained more traditional influences and characteristics within its culinary choices. Religions across both borders are also important factors, as dietary requirements vary between Hindus and Muslims respectively.*"

The region of the foods across West Bengal and Bangladesh is important to consider, as many of the most popular dishes have different variations depending on where you are. In Bangladesh for example, the food can be seen to revolve around Mughlai cuisine, and takes heavy influences from Persian and Arabic cuisine. Bangladeshis use beef, which can be seen in dishes such as the beef kebab, while this meat is not commonly consumed in West Bengal due to religious reasons. Within the southern parts of Bengal that are surrounded by rivers, there is a preference of river fish; central parts favor fried rice and meat, and some of the northern regions prefer vegetable curries.

GEOGRAPHY:

West Bengal is located in the eastern part of India. It is bounded to the north by the state of Sikkim and the country of Bhutan, to the northeast by the state of Assam, to the east by the country of Bangladesh, to the south by the Bay of Bengal, to the southwest by the state of Odisha, to the west by the states of Jharkhand and Bihar, and to the northwest by the country of Nepal.

West Bengal may be broadly divided into two natural geographic divisions—the Gangetic Plain in the south and the sub – Himalayan and Himalayan area in the north. The Gangetic Plain contains fertile alluvial soil deposited by the Ganges (Ganga) River and its tributaries and distributaries. It also features numerous marshes and shallow lakes formed out of dead river courses. While entering West

Bengal the Gnga river is divided in to two, one branch enters Bangladesh as the Padma while the other flows through West Bengal as the Bhagirathi River and Hooghly River in a southern direction. The state capital, Kolkata, is situated on the Hugli in the southern portion of West Bengal. Another important river, the Damodar, joins the Hugli southwest of Kolkata. The elevation of the plain increases slowly toward the west; the rise is most marked near the Chota Nagpur plateau of neighboring Jharkhand.

BRIEF HISTORY:

The earliest mention of Bengal can be found in the old epic of Mahabharta, which has been derived from the Sanskrit word as 'Vanga' or "Banga".

Many dynasties exercised their control over Bengal when monarchy came in fashion in India. In about the 3rd century, Mauryas and Guptas established their rule in Bengal. The establishment of Gupta Empire marked the end of all small kingdoms that flourished in Bengal, ruled by tribal chiefs. The Palas followed the Guptas and established their strong rule in the territory, from about 800 AD till the 11th century, after which the Senas overtook the Empire of Bengal. Sena Dynasty lost the kingdom of Bengal to Qutub – Ud – In – Aibak, the Sultan of Delhi, in the beginning of 13th century. After being a part of Delhi Sultanate, the region of Bengal came under the Mughals in sixteenth century. After the Mughals, history of modern Bengal begins with the advent of the English traders and after the battle of Pallasey in 1757 and battle of Buxar in 1764 they got control of entire Bengal and India, with Calcutta (Kolkata) being the capital. In 1911 the capital was moved to Delhi. In 1971 Bengal was divided into two East Bengal (now Bangladesh) and west Bengal with its capital Kolkata.

CULTURE AND TRADITIONS:

The majority of West Bengal's people live in rural villages. Of those living in urban areas, more than half reside in greater Kolkata. Of the different religions, Hinduism claims the adherence of more than three-fourth of the population. Most of the remainder is Muslim. Throughout the state, Buddhists, Christians, Jains, and Sikhs constitute small minority communities.

Bengali, the main language of the state, is spoken by much of the population. Other languages include Hindi, Santali, Urdu (primarily the language of Muslims), and Nepali (spoken largely in the area of Darjeeling). A small number of people speak Kurukh, the language of the Oraon indigenous group. English, Bengali and Hindi are the language of administration. The people of Bengal live with mutual peace and harmony. Throughout the year there is a festive mood in the state, as each season brings a plethora of festivals along with it. Durga Pooja is celebrated with same joy and grandeur in the state as Id. The cuisines and the culture of West Bengal also demonstrate the inextricable blend of its existent religions.

Bengalis have long fostered art, literature, music, and drama. The visual arts have, by tradition, been based mainly on clay modeling, terra – cotta work, and decorative painting. Bengali literature dates to before the 12th century. The modern period has produced, among others, the Nobel Prize – winning poet Rabindranath Tagore (1861– 1941), whose contribution still dominates the Indian literary scene.

Traditional music takes the form of devotional and cultural songs. Rabindra Sangeet, songs written and composed by Tagore, draw on the pure Indian classical as well as traditional folk – music sources, including the Baul singing genre. The open air theatre or sophisticated. Yatras (jatras) on particular theme are popular. Bengali films have earned national and international awards for their delicate handling of Indian themes; the works of the directors Satyajit Ray, Tapan Sinha, Mrinal Sen, and Aparna Sen are particularly notable. Apart from the religious rituals and ceremonials the people of Bengal or the Bengalis have their own rituals in ceremonies like birth, weddings and even death.

The Gaye holud is a part of a custom of the Bengali wedding and it takes place one or two days prior to the occasion. The Gaye holud is also known as the turmeric function during which haldi is applied on the skin of the bride and the groom for it is believed that turmeric cleanses, soften and brighten the skin, giving the bride's skin the distinctive yellow hue that gives its name to this ceremony. According to Bengalis, the weddings symbolizes purity, sanctity and other good aspects of life. During a wedding ceremony Bengalis do not opt for black color for it is considered as the color of evil whereas they prefer hues of red which signifies luck, emotion and fortune. Banana tree is used to decorate the wedding mandaps and the house for banana tree produces huge number of fruits at a time and so also the couple should be blessed with many children.

A ritual known as Annaprashan is conducted for the babies when it is five to seven months old. This is just to welcome the baby to eat the normal home – made food after it crosses the stage of eating baby food pattern. Bengal had always attracted people of different religions and cultures, and so one can find Gujratis, Marwaris, jains, Muslims, Sikhs, Christians etc. Of the different religions, Hinduism claims the adherence of more than three – fourths of the population. The ruling dynasties, British Empire, post – Independence development and intermingling of people from different backgrounds, physical features have influenced the culture, cuisine and lifestyle of people in Bengal.

CLIMATE:

West Bengal's climate varies from tropical savannah in the southern portions to humid subtropical in the north. The main seasons are summer, rainy season, a short autumn, and winter. While the summer in the delta region is noted for excessive humidity, the western highlands experience a dry summer like northern India, with the highest day temperature ranging from 38 Degree Celsius to 45 Degree Celsius. At nights, a cool southerly breeze carries moisture from the Bay of Bengal. In early summer brief squalls and thunderstorms known as "kal – baisakhi" often arrive from the north or northwest. Monsoons bring rain to the whole state from June to September. West Bengal receives the Bay of Bengal branch of the Indian Ocean monsoon that moves in a northwest direction. For example, Kolkata averages about 64 inches (1,625 mm) per year, of which an average of 13 inches (330 mm) falls in August and less than 1 inch (25 mm) in December. Winter (December–January) is mild over the plains with average minimum temperatures of 15 Degree Celsius. A cold and dry northern wind blows in the winter, substantially lowering the humidity level. However, the Darjeeling Himalayan Hill region experiences a harsh winter, with occasional snowfall at places.

AGRICULTURE AND STAPLE FOOD:

Most of the rural and tribal population is engaged in agricultural activities and cultivation. Rice and fish along with sweets is the staple food of the Bengalis. Around three fourth of West Bengal is agricultural land. Bengal being located at the end point of the rivers, so the soil of this region is very fertile. Bengal owes three times paddy per year and is the largest producer of paddy in India. Almost every village has a large pond where they rear fish according to their need. Every pond is lined by coconut and betel-nut trees. They also raise the boundary of their field during paddy sowing season, fill it with water and rear fish in the field as well. After three months they get good quantity of rice as well as huge amount of fish. The cuisine of West Bengal differs from that of Bangladesh. The Brahmins of Bengal eat fish and no celebration is complete without it. The market is flooded at anytime with all sizes and shapes of carp, salmon, hilsa, bhetki, rui, magur, prawns, koi etc which can be fried, steamed or stewed with curd. Most of the Bengalis will not touch the salt water fish complaining that the fish is not sweet enough. The state is the third largest meat producing state in the country (including poultry) after Uttar Pradesh and Andhra Pradesh. Due to the availability of large green pastoral land, animal rearing is very common. Buffalo and cows are reared in every household and so milk and milk product is abundant.

There were over 40 varieties of rice, 60 kinds of fruits and more than 120 varieties of vegetables in Bengal.

Vegetables included cucumber, carrot, various kinds of gourds, garlic, fenugreek, radish, lotus root, mushroom, eggplant, and green leafy vegetables. Among the fruits Mangoes, coconut, jackfruit, and bananas are widely produced in the southern and central portions of the state. Other foods include peaches, water melon, banana, mango, amalaka (amla), lime, grapes, oranges, pear, jujube, almond, walnuts, coconut, pomegranates, bananas, etc. Spices used in Bengali cooking include turmeric, cinnamon, cardamom, and cloves, ginger, mustard seed, long pepper, poppy seeds, chillies, asafoetida, and sour lemon. Apart from rice potato, jute, sugarcane and wheat are the top five crops of the state. Other major food crops include maize, tobacco, pulses, oil seeds, wheat, barley, and vegetables. The northern areas around Darjeeling and Jalpaiguri have long been known for their production of high – quality tea. Darjeeling region also produces oranges, apples, pineapples, ginger, and cardamom.

CHARACTERISTICS AND SALIENT FEATURES OF THE CUISINE:

- The staple food of Bengal is rice and fish. The fishes commonly used in this cuisine includes Hilsa (Ilish), Carp (Rui), Dried fish (shootki), Indian butter fish (pabda), Clown knife fish (Chitol maach), Mango fish (Topsey), Sea Bass (Bhetki), Prawns / Shrimps (Golda chingri / kucho chingri), Catfish (Tangra / Magur), Perch (koi), Katla. Lightly fermented rice is also used as breakfast in rural and agrarian communities (panta bhat).

- The principal medium of cooking is Shorsher tel (mustard oil). A distinct flavor is imparted to the fish dishes by frying them in mustard oil, before cooking them in the gravy. Shorshe Bata (Mustard paste) is also commonly used for the preparation of gravies.
- Fish is also steamed by the Bengalis (e.g, Bhapa Ilish). The most preferred form of meat in Bengal is mutton, or goat meat. Khashi (castrated goat) or Kochi pantha (kid goat), is also common.
- Special seasonings such as panch phoron – a combination of cumin seeds (jeera), Fennel seeds (mouri), mustard seeds (sorse), methi seeds and onion seeds (kalonjee). Sometimes Celery seeds (radhuni) also become a part of the panch phoron. Radhuni and Poppy seeds (posto) are extensively used in the cuisine.
- The garam masala made up of Cloves (laung), Cinnamon (dalchini), Nutmeg (Jaiphal), Mace (Javitri), small and large cardamom (Elichi) etc.
- The vegetable varieties include kachu or taro (calocasia), lao (bottle gourd) Kumro (pumpkin), Potol (pointed gourd), begun (brinjal), Mulo (radish), Motorshuti (green peas), green like shashni shak, puishak, kachu shak.
- Bengalis also eat flowers like those of bokphul, pumpkin, banana, water reeds, tender drumsticks and peels of potato or pumpkin.
- A lunch consists of Rice, Bhaja (assorted fried items including vegetables and fish), Leafy vegetable – Saag (palong saag, Pui saag, Lal saag etc), Sukto, various dals (lentil) such as Moong, Masoor, Beuli (Urad), Arhar, Cholar(Chana) dal etc, followed by different Vegetarian preparations, Fish and Meat (Chicken or Mutton) preparations. This is followed by the Chutney and papad

and finally the sweets of which there are endless mouth watcring varieties such as Rosogolla, Sandesh, Misti doi, Rabri, Mihidana, Sitabhog, Rajbhog, Kamalabhog, Kalakad etc

- Roti, Paratha, Luchi are also common.
- The very common snacks include the ―Jhal moori‖ various kinds of Telebhaja (Chops – vegetable, egg etc, Beguni, Peyazi), kachudi, singhada, egg roll, chicken roll, puckha (puffed mini stuffed with mashed potato and dipped in tamarind water), nimkis (maida dough rice with black onion seeds shaped into triangles and deep fried), chanachur etc.
- Sweet Dishes reflect a special culinary expertise of the state and the variety is one of the largest in the global culinary spectacle. The most common ones include – Rosogolla, Sandesh (Narompak – soft or korapak – hard), Misti doi, Rabri, Mihidana, Sitabhog, Rajbhog, Kamalabhog, Kalakad, Chum chum, Jolbhora, ladycanny/ladykini, Chaler payash, Chenar payash, darbesh, Malpoa, shor bhaja, langcha etc. The two basic ingredients of Bengali sweets are sugar and milk. The milk is thickened either by boiling it down to make a thick liquid called khoa, or by curdling it with lemon juice or yogurt to produce curds, called channa. Sugar is not the only ingredient with which the sweetness is imparted in the sweets, various jaggery (gur) which includes patali gur, khejur gur (date jaggey) etc. The main body of the sweets are mostly made of coconut, til seeds, rice, rice flour, refined flour etc apart from Chenna.
- Traditional home made delicacies include various kinds of Pitha (a pancake like sweet base of semolina or flour

which is rolled around a variety of fillings like coconut and kheer and fried in ghee – chandrapuli, gokul, pati shapta, chitai piṭha, aski pithe, muger puli and dudh puli). Pithas are usually made from rice or wheat flour mixed with sugar, jaggery, grated coconut etc. These are usually enjoyed with the sweet syrups of Khejur gur (Date tree molasses)/ they are usually fried or steamed – the most common ones include bhapapitha (steamed), Pakanpitha (fried) and Pulipitha (dumplings)

- Moa (flat rice or puffed rice bound with jaggery cooked to a correct degree and then made into dumplings). Another popular kind of moa is Jaynagarer Moa, a moya particularly made in Jaynagar, South 24 Parganas district, Paschimbanga (West Bengal) which uses khoi and a sugar – milk – spices mixture as binder. Moas are made specially during winter.
- Naru (Grated coconut or til seeds bound with cooked jiggery or sugar and formed into dumplings) etc.
- Aamsotto (thickened mango pulp) is another homemade delicacy.
- A day begins with moori (puffed rice) with potatoes, cucumber, green chilli and mustard oil, tea or milk.

A typical Bengali meal structure:

The procession of tastes at a meal runs from a bitter start to a sweet finish.

- To start with, especially at lunch, is Sukto.
- Rice is first savoured with ghee, salt and green chillis, then comes dhal accompanied by fried vegetables

(bhaja) or boiled vegetables (bhate), followed by spiced vegetables like dalna or ghonto.

- Then comes fish preparations, first lightly – spiced ones like maccher jhol, and then those more heavily spiced.
- This would be followed by a sweet – sour ambal or tauk (chutney) and fried papads. The chutney is typically tangy and sweet; usually made of aam (mangoes), tomatoes, anarôsh (pineapple), tetul (tamarind), pepe (papaya), or just a combination of fruits and dry fruits called mixed fruit chutney served in biye badi (marriage).
- A dessert of mishti – doi (sweet curds), accompanied by dry sweets, or of payesh, accompanied by fruits like the mango, will end the meal, with paan (betel leaves) as a terminal digestive.
- Traditionally meals were served on a bell – metal thala (plate) and in the batis (bowls, except for the sour items). The night meal omits shukto and could include luchis, a palao and a dalna of various delicately spiced vegetables.

Common Bengali cooking styles –

- **Ambal**– A sour dish made either with several vegetables or with fish, the sourness being produced by the addition of tamarind pulp.
- **Bhaja**– Anything fried, either by itself or in batter.
- **Bhapa**– Fish or vegetables steamed with oil and spices. A classic steaming technique is to wrap the fish in banana leaf to give it a faint musky, smoky scent.

- **Bhate** – Any vegetable, such as potatoes, beans, pumpkins or even dal, first boiled whole and then mashed and seasoned with mustard oil or ghee and spices.
- **Bhuna**– A term of Urdu origin, meaning fried for a long time with ground and whole spices over high heat. Usually applied to meat.
- **Dalna** – Mixed vegetables (*echor*) or eggs, cooked in a medium thick gravy seasoned with ground spices, ginger especially *garom mashla* (hot spices) and a touch of ghee.
- **Dom**– Vegetables, especially potatoes, or meat, cooked over a covered pot slowly over a low heat.
- **Ghanto** – Different complementary vegetables (e.g., cabbage, green peas, potatoes or banana blossom, coconut, chickpeas) are chopped or finely grated and cooked with both a phoron and ground spices. Dried pellets of dal (*boris*) are often added to the *ghanto*. Ghee is commonly added at the end. Non – vegetarian ghantos are also made, with fish or fish heads added to vegetables. The famous *murighanto* is made with fish heads cooked in a fine variety of rice. Some ghantos are very dry while others a thick and juicy.
- **Jhal**– Literally, hot. A great favorite in West Bengali households, this is made with fish or shrimp or crab, first lightly fried and then cooked in a light sauce of ground red chilli or ground mustard and a flavoring of panch – phoron or kala jeera. Being dryish it is often eaten with a little bit of dal pored over the rice.
- **Jhol** – A light fish or vegetable stew seasoned with ground spices like ginger, cumin, coriander, chilli and turmeric with pieces of fish and longitudinal slices of vegetables floating in it. The gravy is thin yet extremely

flavourful. Whole green chillies are usually added at the end and green coriander leaves are used to season for extra taste.

- **Kalia**– A very rich preparation of fish, meat or vegetables using a lot of oil and ghee with a sauce usually based on ground ginger and onion paste and garom mashla.
- **Koftas**(or *Boras*) – Ground meat or vegetable croquettes bound together by spices and/or eggs served alone or in savoury gravy.
- **Korma** – Another term of Urdu origin, meaning meat or chicken cooked in mild yoghurt based gravy with ghee instead of oil.
- **Kassa** – This is a way of cooking for specially red meats like lamb or mutton is bhunoad in a very thick spicy masala of onion, ginger, garlic, chilli powder, turmeric powder and cumin powder and made into a gravy sort.
- **Pora**– Literally, burnt. Vegetables are wrapped in leaves and roasted over a wood or charcoal fire. Some, like eggplants (brinjals/aubergines), are put directly over the flames. Before eating the roasted vegetable is mixed with oil and spices.
- **Phoron** – It is predominantly the kind of tempering, which is used in the preparation of lentils, with various lentils having their own tempering.
- **Gotasheddho** –fruits and half boiled vegetables offered to goddess Saraswati during Saraswati Puja.
- **Dolma or Patoler Dolma**– The name is coming from Turkey, but the food is different. The vegetable Patol is stuffed either with a combination of grated coconut, chickpeas, etc. or more commonly with fish and then fried. The fish is boiled with turmeric and salt, then bones are removed and then onion, ginger and garam

masala are fried in oil and boiled fish is added and churned to prepare the stuffing.

- **Paturi**– Typically fish, seasoned with spices (usually shorshe) wrapped in banana leaves and steamed or roasted over a charcoal fire.
- **Polau**– Fragrant dish of rice with ghee, spices and small pieces of vegetables. Long grained aromatic rice is usually used, but some aromatic short grained versions such as Kalijira or Gobindobhog may also be used.
- **Tarakri** – A general term often used in Bengal the way `curry` is used in English. Originally from Persian, the word first meant uncooked garden vegetables. From this it was a natural extension to mean cooked vegetables or even fish and vegetables cooked together.
- **Chorchori** – Usually a vegetable dish with one or more varieties of vegetables cut into longish strips, sometimes with the stalks of leafy greens added, all lightly seasoned with spices like mustard or poppy seeds and flavoured with a phoron. The skin and bone of large fish like *bhetki or chitol* can be made into a chachchari called kanta – chachchari, *kanta, meaning fish – bone.*
- **Chhanchra** – A combination dish made with different vegetables, portions of fish head and fish oil (entrails).
- **Chhenchki** – Tiny pieces of one or more vegetable – or, sometimes even the peels (of potatoes, lau, pumpkin or patol for example) – usually flavored with panch – phoron or whole mustard seeds or kala jeera. Chopped onion and garlic can also be used, but hardly any ground spices.
- **Chop**– Croquettes, usually coated with crushed biscuit or breadcrumbs.
- **Shukto** – This is a dish that is essential bitter, made up of neem or other bitter leaves, bitter gourd, brinjals,

potatoes, radish and green bananas, with spices like turmeric, ginger, mustard and radhuni (celery seed) pastes.

- Shak– Any kind of green leafy vegetable, like spinach and mustard greens, often cooked till just wilted in a touch of oil and tempering of nigela seeds.

Bengali breads –

Though Bengalis, primarily loves to eat rice, yet there are a few typical Bengali Breads, which are quite famous in various parts of Bengal. Some of the prominent among these are –

- Luchi –Eaten for mainly snacks, equivalent to the north Indian poories (the difference is that luchi is made out of refined flour and fried without colour) and taken very commonly with cholar dal tempered with coconut.
- Khasta Luchi – The dough is much richer with fat and flaky. Hence, known as khasta kachuri.
- Porotha –It is a kind of flaky bread, made out of whole wheat flour and is essentially triangular in shape.
- Roti –Whole wheat flour bread, toasted on griddle.
- Radhabollobbi –An urad dal stuffed poori made out of whole wheat flour normally had with *aloo dom*.
- Dhakai porotha –Flaky, layered bread from Dhaka in Bangladesh.
- Matter (green peas) kachuri – Flaky bread, stuffed with matar (green peas) paste and deep – fried. Heing is commonly used in the green peas mixture.

EQUIPMENTS AND UTENSILS USED:

- Bonti – A curved raised blade attached to a long, flat cutting vegetables, fish and meat. The bonti used for fish and meat is kept separate from vegetable bonti and the non – veg ansh – bonti (ansh implies scales of fish).
- Haadi –A cooking pot with a rounded bottom slightly narrowed at the neck with a wide rim to facilitate holding, while draining excess of rice water.
- Dekchi –Referred as saucepan without a handle, usually of greater depth. Used for boiling, sautéing
- Karai –A cooking pot shaped like a Chinese wok, but much deeper. Used for deep frying, stir – frying as well as for preparations and sauces and gravy. It's usually made of iron or aluminium and usually has two – looped handles.
- Tawa –It's a griddle, used for making porothas.
- Thala –A circular plate of authentically brass, but nowadays of steel, on which food is served.
- Khunti –Long handled implement of steel or iron with a flat thin belt – shaped piece, used as stirrers (metal spatula).
- Hatha –A metal spoon with indention, used as stirrers and also for transferring food stuffs (ladle).
- Sarashi –equipment, used for holding vessels hot on range.
- Chakni –A sieve.
- Chamuch –A spoon.
- Jhanjri – perforated spoon
- Sheelnora –Grinding stone, slab of 16 inches by 10 inches and a small bolster – shaped stone roller 9 inches long. Both the slab and roller are chipped from time to

time as they are worn smooth.

- HamalDista –Motar and pestle, which could be used in place of sheelnora. Usually used for grinding spices to a fine powder or to a fine paste with the addition of water.
- Dhenki– A long wooden board mounted on a short pedestal, in the middle, much like a see – saw. The tradition Bengali instrument of taking the husk off the rice.
- Ghutni– It is a wooden hand blender used for pureeing lentils and sauces. Jhanjri– It is a large wire meshed flat spoon used for deep frying fish or breads.
- Belunchaki– Round pastry board and rolling pin.
- Kuruni– It is a uni – tasker, to grate coconuts.

Influence of the widows:

In medieval Bengal the treatment of Hindu widows was much more restrictive than was common elsewhere and lived under strict dietary restrictions. They were usually not allowed any interests but religion and housework, so the kitchen was an important part of their lives; traditional cuisine was deeply influenced by them.

Their ingenuity and skill led to many culinary practices; simple spice combinations, the ability to prepare small quantities (since widows often ate alone) and creative use of the simplest of cooking techniques. Since widows were banned 'impassioning' or aphrodisiac condiments such as onion or garlic, most traditional Bengali vegetarian recipes don't use them; this is in stark contrast to the rest of the Indian subcontinent where almost every dish calls for onions and garlic. This has led to a definite slant towards ginger in Bengali vegetarian food, and even in many common fish dishes.

Serving and Eating Bengali Food:

The Bengali people are perhaps the greatest food lovers in the Indian subcontinent. A Bengali meal of many items which requires long hours of labour and skill in the kitchen has long been a major part of culture of West Bengal. The traditional way of serving food is on the floor, where individual pieces of carpet, called asans, are spread for each person to sit on. In front of this seat is placed a large plate (thala) made of bell metal/steel or on a large piece of fresh cut banana leaf.

Around this plate a number of small metal or earthen bowls (bati) are placed in which portions of dal, vegetables, fish, meat chutney and dessert are served. In the centre of the plate a small mound of piping hot rice kept surrounded by fried vegetables, lemon wedges, whole green chillies, little salt. Finally in the centre of the mound of rice a little hole is made to pour in a spoonful of ghee to flavour the initial mouthfuls of rice. Bengalis eat everything with their fingers. It is helpful to pick out thin bones of fish like hilsa.

Apart from this purposeful aspect, the fingers also provide an awareness of texture which becomes as important as that felt by the tongue. The various mashed vegetables or different rice or varieties of fish we eat are all appreciated by the fingers before they enter the mouth. The most important style of eating in Bengal cuisine is eating each dish separately with a little bit of rice in order to relish its individual taste. The more delicate tastes always come first and it is only by graduating from these to stronger ones that you can accommodate the whole range of taste.

Vegetables, especially the bitter ones, are the first item followed by dal, fries or fritters of fish and vegetables. After this comes any of the complex vegetable dishes like ghanto or chachchari, followed by the important Machher jhol as well as other fish preparations. Meat will always follow fish, and chutneys and ambals will provide the stimulating touch of sourness to make the tongue expect the sweet dishes. Varieties of sweets and sweet curd are served. Last item perhaps would be sweet betel leaf (pan).

SPECIALTIES DURING FESTIVALS AND OTHER OCCASIONS:

- Cutlet: Very different from the Cutlets of the Brits, this is referred typically to a crumb coated thinly spread out dough, made generally of chicken/mutton minced, mixed together with onion, bread crumbs and chillies. Generally it is then dipped in egg and coated in breadcrumb, fried and served with thin julienne of cucumber, carrots, radish and onions. Often an egg mixed with a teaspoon or two water and a pinch of salt is dropped on top of the frying cutlet, to make it into a "Kabiraji" the Bengali pronunciation of a "Coverage" Cutlet, influenced by the British.

- Aloo posto: Potatoes are cooked in freshly ground poppy seed paste and flavoured with diffetent spices and turmeric.

- Kobiraji cutlet: This preparation is made from the chicken breast which is marinated with turmeric, salt, ginger and garlic paste, onion paste, green chillies and red chilli powder. The marinated chicken is coated in alight batter of rice flour and eggs and deep fat fried until golden brown.

- Dhokar dalna: A gram flour batter is cooked with spices and then spread on a tray and steamed. It is then cut into small pieces in the shape of a diamond and deep – fat fried. The fried dumplings are now stewed in a gravy of boiled onion paste, thickened with gram flour and whole spices.

- Kasha mangsho: This is a semi – dry preparation of the lamb that gets a unique dark colour from the iron kadhai in which it is cooked and caramelized sugar. This can be had with luchi.

- Doi maach: This is a classical preparation of Bengal in which the fish is stewed in a yoghurt based gravy.

- Chingri malai curry: The preparation is a speciality of the cuisine and is normally prepared during the special occasions. Prawns are stewed in a gravy made with boiled onion paste, thickened with coconut milk with a touch of red chilli powder and turmeric.

- Chitol Macher muitha: Chitol is a fish specially consumed during the Durga puja. The meat from the back part after removing the bones is shaped into koftas and simmered into a gravy.

- Payeesh: rice cooked in milk (Kheer).

- Shingara: Like the North Indian Samosa, only smaller, filling can vary right from potato, cauliflower, and peas to mutton mince.

- Deem er Devil: Or egg chop –Hard boiled egg coated with a spicy potato mash, egg washed and rolled in bread crumbs and deep fried. Served with Dhone Chutney (Coriander Chutney).

- Bhetki Mach er Chop: Fillets of Bhetki fish coated with mashed potatoes and coriander chutney, egg washed and rolled in bread crumbs and shallow fried.

- Moglai Paratha: A stuffed bread made of whole wheat flour, stuffed with Masala Mutton Kheema, shallow fried and served with Potato Curry, Onion Rings, Coriander Chutney and Lemon Wedges.

- Chicken Kabiraji: Chicken Joints having a coating of fluffy egg whites and bread crumbs served with Coriander Chutney, Onion Rings and Lemon Wedges.

- Mochar Chop: Banana Flowers mixed with mashed potatoes, rolled in bread crumbs and deep fried.

- Shukto: Vegetable preperation includingBitter Gourd, Ridge Gourd, Raw Bananas, Brinjal, String Beans, Potato, in a Poppy Seed and Mustar Paste with a Bengal tempering of Panch Phoron, Bay Leaves and Hing.

- Doi Potol: Doi Potol or Pointed Gourd cooked with curd is a rich recipe with thick gravy, usually served in special occasion as a vegetarian alternative to spicy meat dishes. Doi potol demonstrate the richness of Bengali Cuisine to the fullest.

- Thor Chhechhki: Banana Stem flavored with panch – phoron or whole mustard seeds or kala jeera. Chopped onion and garlic can also be used, but hardly any ground spices.

- Jhinge Aloo Poshtu: Ridge Gourd and Potatoes cooked in a Poppy Seed Paste flavoured with Panch Phoron and Green Chilles.

- Shorshe Ilish: A spicy Hilsa fish preparation made with Hilsa fish and mustard paste. It is pungent if the mustard paste is not cooked well and can hit your throat if you eat too much of it.

- Bhetki Paturi: Bhetki fish marinated with Mustard Paste, Ginger Garlic Paste, Green Chilly Paste, Mustard Oil, Wrapped in Plantain Leaf and then kept in pan till the leaves are browned well.

- Daab Chingri: Prawns flavoured with panch phoron and cooked in a tender coconut shell.

- Rui Mach er Kaaliya: A very rich preparation of Rahu Fish using a lot of oil and ghee with a sauce usually based on ground ginger and onion paste and garam masala.

- Pabda Macher Jhal: Literally, hot. A great favorite in West Bengali households, this is made with Indian Butter Fish, first lightly fried and then cooked in a light sauce of ground red chilli or ground mustard and a flavoring of panch – phoron or kala jeera. Being dryish it is often eaten with a little bit of dal pored over the rice.

- Ilish Macher Dim Diye Ambol: A sour dish made with Hilsa Roe, the sourness being produced by the addition of tamarind pulp.

- Mourola Macher Bhaja: A very small fish like sardines, deep fried.

- Tangra Macher Jhol: Tangra fish cooked with kalonji. Very liquidy gravy and light flavour. Usually had when a person is sick

- Muri Ghonto: dry dish made with fried fish head (known as maacher matha or muro in Bengali), potatoes, very little rice and myriad spices. Don't turn up your nose, it smells nothing but heavenly and tastes more so.

- Murgir Jhol: A simple Chicken Curry cooked with potatoes and lots of gravy.

- Kasha Mangsho: Mutton Sauteed with spices and masalas with very little addition of water. Best had with Roomali Roti or Luchi.

- Lao Chingri: A simple preparation made with Bottle Gourd and shrimps.

- Luchi: Deep fried Flat bread made with a mixture of refined flour, water and ghee.

- Karausutir Kachori: Deep Fried Round Flat bread made with whole wheat flour and has peas as a filling. Ideal for breakfast when served with Potato Curry and Jalebi.

- Radhaballavi: It is stuffed deep fried bread. It is stuffed with lentil and little spices. It is a must on the menu of every ceremony such as marriages, birthdays etc.

- Roshogolla: The dish is made from balls of chhena (an Indian cottage cheese) and semolina dough, cooked in sugar syrup.

- Roshmalai: Ras malai consists of sugary, cream to yellow – colored balls (or flattened balls) of paneer soaked in malai (clotted cream) flavored with cardamom.

- Mishti Aloor Pantua: Sweet Potato Balls in Sugar Syrup. It is a variation of such pantuas, where we substitute the regular semolina, ghee, milk and khoya with sweet potatoes.

- Chom Chom: Like Rasgulla but dryer made with Cottage Cheese, Refined Flour, Cardamom Powder, Condensed Milk, Saffron and Sugar.

- Sita Bhog: Known as Sita Bhog as Goddess Sita liked it, made with a mixture of Rice Flour, Refined Flour, Cottage Cheese, Cardamom Powder, Rose Essence and Sugar. Made in the shape of long rice grains and served at room temperature.

- Lal Mishti Doi: It is prepared by boiling milk until it is slightly thickened, sweetening it with sugar, either gura (brown sugar) or khajuri gura (date molasses), and allowing the milk to ferment overnight. Earthenware is always used as the container for making mitha dahi because the gradual evaporation of water through its porous walls not only further thickens the yoghurt, but also produces the right temperature for the growth of the culture. Very often the yoghurt is delicately seasoned with a hint of elaach (cardamoms) for fragrance.

- Bhaapa Doi: Bhapa Doi is an unsweetened Bengali dessert which is essentially steamed yoghurt. It has the texture and consistency of soft cheesecake. It has a sweet, mild taste.

- Pathishapta: Patishapta is actually a rice flour crepe with coconut and jaggery fillings.

- Puli Peethe Payesh: Rice Flour Dumplings with a filling of Rice Kheer and then put in thickened sweet milk (Payesh)

- Sandesh: It is created with milk and sugar. Some recipes of Sandesh call for the use of chhana (curdled milk) or paneer instead of milk

- Rajbhog: Saffron flavoured Rasgullas with a dry fruit filling.

- Chenna Jilebi: Fresh chhena is thoroughly kneaded and rolled up into shapes similar to pretzels, before being deep fried. The fully fried chhena pretzels are then soaked in a sugary syrup. Chhena jalebis are served either hot or chilled.

- Kachgolla: Like Rasgulla but less sweet, and coated with desiccated coconut.

- Chenna Payesh: Kheer Made with Cottage Cheese.

- Potol Mishti: Steamed Parwal, with a filling of Mawa, Cardamom Powder, simmered in Sugar Syrup and then covered with Silver Foil.

- Jhal – Muɾi: One of the most popular and iconic snack foods of Bengal, jhal literally means 'hot' or 'spicy'. Jhal – muɾi is puffed rice with spices, vegetables and raw mustard oil. Depending on what is added, there are many kinds of jhal muɾi but the most common is a bhôrta made of chopped shallot, jira roasted ground cumin, bitnoon black salt lôngka / morich chilis (either kacha 'ripe' or shukna 'dried'), mustard oil, dhone pata (fresh coriander leaves) and mudhi.

- Begun Bhaja: Brinjal fritters

- Mochar Ghonto: It is a traditional Bengali preparation, where the banana flowers are cooked along with potato and aromatic spices.

- Kanchkolar Kofta: Kofta curry made with raw bananas.

- Kasundi: Mustard paste

FESTIVITIES:

- **Durga Puja–** This festival happens in the period between September and October. Durga Puja is one of the major festivals of West Bengal. The massive celebration that happens during the festival is famous throughout the world. It commemorates the triumph of Good over Evil. People have this belief that Goddess Durga defeated the demon *Mahishasura* after a fierce battle that lasted for ten days. The last day or tenth day is called as *Vijay Dashmi*. This festival is marked by offering prayers to the Goddess Durga, rejoicing, feasts, dance, drama and music. On this auspicious day, people dress up in new colorful clothes. They visit puja pandals of different communities and pay reverence to the ten – armed goddess Durga. In the pandals, Goddess Saraswati, Goddess Lakshmi, Lord Ganesha, and Kartikeya are beautifully ornated and decorated. The priests do the prayers at prearranged times whereas the devotees visit pandals during the day. Stalls selling Jhal muri, cutlet, chop, mughlai porotha can be seen around nearby pandal.

- **Poush Sankranti** – In West Bengal, Makar Sankranti is celebrated as— Poush Sankranti‖. The name of the festival is derived from the Bengali month 'Poush'. It is the month when this harvest festival is celebrated. The newly collected paddy along with the date palm syrup as Patali and Khejurer Gur is used to prepare a rich variety of conventional Bengali sweets. These sweets are made with coconut, rice flour, date palm jaggery, and milk. Peethe (A Rice Flour Dumpling filled with Kheer and then put in Payesh) is also served.

- **Dol Purnima**– Hindu festival that is celebrated with a different name in West Bengal state is Dol-Purnima.

This is the Bengali version of the Holi festival. Dol Purnima is celebrated by men and women in a very dignified manner.On the early morning of the Dol Purnima day, the students get themselves dressed up in pure white clothes or saffron – colored dress. They also wear fresh garlands of scented flowers. Everyone enjoys this occasion by immersing themselves completely in singing and dancing on the beats of musical instruments. Different types of musical instruments are used such as dubri, ektara, veena, etc. The devotees swing the idols and women sing devotional songs and dance around the swing. During these activities, the men spray colored powder, abir and colored water at them. Doi Rui, Mochar Tarkari, Dhokar Dalna, mutton curry, coconut gujia, Muri – ghonto etc are some of the festive favorite.

- **Jamai Shoshti**– This is a beautiful and distinctive festival that commemorates the relationship between a son in law and mother in law. This day brings the warmth back in their relationship. Jamai is a term that refers to the 'son in law'. The Jamai Shoshti festival is celebrated in May or June. On this day, the son in law goes to her mother in law and seeks her blessing for a prosperous future. A grand celebration is organized on this day to welcome the arrival of a son in law to their house. Radhaballavi and cholar dal, Mishti pulao, Kosha mansho, Bhetki, Rosogolla, Sandesh are some of the favourites. The ritual happens in the presence of close members of the household. As per the tradition, the mother in law prepares a variety of mouth – watering and delectable Bengali dishes and gives gifts to her son in law.

- **Chhat Puja–** Chhath is a primitive Hindu festival. It is the only Vedic festival that is dedicated to the Surya Dev, Sun God, and ChhathiMaiya (Goddess Usha mentioned in Vedic scriptures). The Chhath Puja is performed to pay gratitude to Lord Surya to sustain life on earth. While performing the rituals of this festival, people request the Lord to grant them a few wishes. In Hindu scriptures, it is mentioned that worship to Lord Sun helps in curing various types of ailments that include leprosy. It also assists in ensuring the prosperity and longevity of friends, family members, and elders. Thekua, Poori, Hara chana, Rasiyaw, tilkut are some specialty served during this festival.

- **Id – Ul – Fitr–** Eid is another very significant festival in West Bengal. It is celebrated mostly by the Muslims in the state. The date of the occurrence of this festival isn't fixed. Id – Ul – Fitr is celebrated in May. It comes after the break of the auspicious Ramzan month. This festival memorializes the commencement of a joyful – communion post a month of fasting and prayer. Haleem, Biriyani, Nehari, simai, mishit doi, Bakarkhani are some of the mouthwatering especialities prepared and served during this festival.

- **Bhai Phota–** Bhai Phota is celebrated throughout West Bengal in the month of November. This festival is celebrated in Kolkata as a substitute for the Hindu Raksha Bandhan although it is somewhat different. In this, the sister puts a *'tika'* on the forehead of her brother while muttering incantations and then feeds him, sweets. The sister prays for the long life of her brother and also that he finds the strength to fight wrongdoings. This is the Bengali version of celebration cherishes the bond between a brother and sister.

- **Poila Boishakh**– Poila Boishakh or the first day of Baisakh is the first day of a Bengali calendar year which usually falls on the 14th or 15th of April. The day is often known as Bengali New Year. This day marks the beginning of a new year for a Bengali household and thus calls for a celebration. People make extensive preparations for this day, buying new clothes, preparing extensive dishes at home and most importantly offering prayers to Gods and Goddesses. This day is very special for the Bengalis. On this day the traders start their new accounting books, the ceremony is commonly known as 'Hal Khata'.

- **Kali Puja**– Kali Puja is another noteworthy festival that takes place in West Bengal in October or November. This is a long festival that goes for about twenty days. It happens after Durga Puja. Besides Durga Puja, it is one of the largest festivals of Kolkata. Kali Puja festival is celebrated in the honor of Goddess Kali. It is recognized by the chanting of mantras in the nighttime that goes till dawn. The Goddess is ornated with beautiful garlands made of hibiscuses. All the sacred chanting of mantras is carried out in the presence of the holy fire. Devotees offer several types of offerings to the Goddess that includes sweets, lentils, and rice. The street is full oif stalls serving Rolls and chowmein, Manshor jhol, Sorsher maach, Devil egg, Egg roll, Jhal muri etc.

- **Lakshmi Puja**– Lakshmi Puja is another very significant Hindu festival celebrated by the Bengalis in October. It is celebrated throughout the state with great enthusiasm and passion. During this festival, people from different parts of the world come to visit the state to be a part of this grand festivity. Lakshmi Puja takes place a week later Vijay Dashmi.People devote their respect and gratitude towards Maa Lakshmi who is believed to be the Goddess of prosperity, and wealth. Lakshmi Pooja is the festival of lights. People celebrate it at home by either performing all the rituals by a priest or on their own. Prayers are made to bestow prosperity and wealth to their homes.

- **GangaSagar Mela** – Ganga Sagar Mela, also known as Ganga Dussehra Mela is held in the month of January, on the occasion of Makar Sankranti at Sagardwip, about 105 km. south of Kolkata. Sagardwip is the island situated at the mouth of Ganga where the Hugli river joins the sea. This is the largest fair of the West Bengal and celebrated for three days. On this day, a large number of Hindu pilgrims collect here and take bath in the holy waters and visit the Kapil Muni Temple.

- **Christmas** – Christmas or Christmas Day meaning "Christ's Mass" is an annual festival commemorating the birth of Jesus Christ, observed most commonly on December 25 as a religious and cultural celebration among billions of people around the world. A feast central to the Christian liturgical year, it is prepared for by the season of Advent or Nativity Fast and is prolonged by the Octave of Christmas and further by the season of Christmastide. Christmas Day is a public holiday in many of the world's nations is celebrated culturally by a large number of non – Christian people, and is an integral part of the Christmas and holiday season.

Recipes from Bengal:

Doi Machh

Ingredients

- Rohu fish – 1 kg
- Curd – 250 gm
- Turmeric – ¼ tsp
- Red chili pdr – 5 gm
- Onions – 200 gm
- Corn flour – 25 gm
- Ginger – 5 gm
- Salt – tt
- Garlic – 10 gm
- Cinnamon – 5 gm
- Cardamom – 5 gm
- Cloves – 5 gm
- Bay leaves
- Fat – 50 gm
- Gr. chili – 5 gm

Method

- Clean and cut rohu or any other water fish into large pieces.
- Apply salt and turmeric, set aside for ½ hour.
- Heat oil and shallow fry the fish and keep aside.

- Combine together curd, turmeric, corn flour, chili pdr. ½ the onion, ginger, garlic (all finely ground).
- Soak the fish in the above mixture.
- Heat fats slightly, fry the rest of sliced onions.
- Add whole cinnamon, cardamom, cloves, bay leaves and gr. Chilies.
- Add fish and allow simmering for 15 minutes. Check for salt and remove.

Panch Phoroner Charchari

Ingredients

- Potatoes – 225 gm
- Brinjal – 115 gm
- Red pumpkin – 115 gm
- Peas – 115 gm
- Gr. chilies – 10 gm
- Kalaunji – 5 gm
- Mustard – 5 gm
- Cumin – 5 gm
- Methi – 5 gm
- Fennel – 5 gm
- Curry leaves – 1 sprig
- Sugar – pinch
- Oil – 15 ml
- Salt – tt
- Red chili – 1 no

Method

- Peel and cut the potatoes and pumpkin into 1 – inch cubes.
- Cut brinjals into small pieces and shell peas.
- Heat fat and fry the red chilies broken into pieces, slit green chilies, panch phoran and curry leaves.
- When they begin to crackle add the vegetables and sauté.
- Add salt, sugar and enough water to cook the vegetables.
- Simmer till the vegetables are cooked and tender and most of the water is evaporated.

Sukto

Ingredients

- Raw banana – 150 no
- Radish - 150 gm
- Potato – 100 gm
- Brinjal – 100 gm
- Bitter gourd – 100 gm
- Mustard seeds– 1 ½ tbsp.
- Fenugreek seeds– ½ tsp.
- Posto(poppy seeds – 2 tbsp
- Salt – to taste

Method

- Soak 1 tbsp. of each mustard seeds and poppy seeds in warm water. Cut plantain, radish, potato and eggplant lengthwise (about 2" long). Heat 1/4 cup of oil in a wok.

Fry the eggplant pieces, set aside.

- Fry the bittergourd slices, and set aside. In the remaining oil, roast 1/2 tsp. each of fenugreek seeds and mustard seeds. When mustard seeds start to pop, add to it the plantain, radish(mulo), and potato and stir fry in medium heat. As you stir the vegetables, blend the soaked mustard seeds and poppy seeds and about 1" long fresh ginger root, all in a blender into a smooth paste.
- After stir frying vegetables for about 5 to 7 minutes, add the blended mixture to the vegetables and stir constantly for about 2 minutes.
- Add salt. Also, add the fried bitter gourd slices and eggplant pieces. Add now to the "shukto" about 1/2 cup of hot water and cover wok for about 5 minutes, stirring occasionally and check if the vegetables are cooked or not.
- When vegetables are all cooked, pour on top about 1 tsp. of either butter or ghee. Serve with rice.

Ghee Bhaat

Ingredients

- Basmati rice – 500 gm
- Almonds – 10 gm
- Pista – 10gm
- Raisins – 10 gm
- Khoya – 25 gm
- Cloves – 4 nos
- Cinnamon – 5 gm
- Cardamom – 5 gm

- Saffron – few strands
- Nutmeg – pinch
- Mace – 2 blades
- Cumin – 2 gm
- Shahi jeera – 2 gm
- Ghee – 50 gm
- Salt – tt
- Peppercorn – 6 no

Method

- Tie in a muslin cloth all the spices and boil the water for ½ hours.Pick, wash and drain the rice.
- Dissolve saffron in little warm water.
- Heat the fat and fry the nuts, remove.
- In the same fat fry rice, add the spiced water, boil and cook the rice till tender.
- Add khoya, saffron, cover for few minutes and lastly pour the remaining ghee.
- Keep covered for few minutes and the mix well.
- Serve garnished with nuts and raisins.

Ledigini

Ingredients

- Khoya – 100 gm
- Paneer – 50 gm
- Sugar – 150 gm
- Cardamom – pinch
- Maida – 15 gm
- Rose essence – few drops

- Soda – bi – carb – pinch
- Fat – to fry
- Bay leaf – 2 nos

Method

- Prepare the sugar syrup of one string consistency – adding bay leaf.
- Add fewer drops of rose essence.
- Pass mawa and paneer through a sieve, add crushed cardamom and soda – bi – carb, maida and very little amount of water and make soft dough. (Do not knead too much).
- Divide into small portions and roll into small round balls.
- Deep – fry the balls on moderate fire to golden brown stirring constantly by moving the kadai or with a flat spoon. When the gulab jamun is done they will automatically float on top.
- Drain well and add to the prepared sugar syrup, let the syrup be absorbed and then serve.

CHAPTER SEVEN

SUMMARY

Indo-Gangetic Plain, also known as the North Indus Plain, stretches to the west (including) from the Brahmaputra River Valley and Ganges (Ganga), to the Indus River Valley, from the North Indian Plain, a large north-central portion of the Indian subsoil region. The region includes affluent and most populated regions of the subcontinent. Most of the plain is comprised of alluvial soil formed by the three major rivers and their tributaries. Weak rainfall or drought in winter arise in the eastern portion of the region, but in the summer rainfall are so extreme that large areas become swamps or freshwater lakes. The plain eventually dries to the west where the Thar Desert incorporated.

"The Indo-Gangetic Plains are found in the states of Punjab, Haryana, Uttar Pradesh, Bihar and West Bengal and consist of two major drainage basins: the drainage basin Punjab and Haryana, and the drainage basin Ganges-Brahmaputra. The entire Plain is between 400-800 km wide and is now a sinking basin due to seismic changes in the earth. The land is highly fertile due to the nature of the Indo-Gangetic Plains, and is thus suitable for farming activities."

Delhi, Lucknow, Patna, Varanasi, Kolkata and Chandigarh are some notable cities situated here. These regions are considered among the most extensively farmed in the whole world, consisting mostly of wheat and rice cultivation. Some other traditional crops are also found in these regions, however, such as cotton, corn, and sugarcane. The region has an incredibly high population density as a result of this expanded cultivation and almost one hundred crore people actually live here.

Dividing the entire area into 5 separate sub-regions. Regions 1 and 2 are spread around Pakistan, Haryana and Punjab, Regions 3 and 4 inhabit Uttar Pradesh, Bihar and Nepal and lastly West Bengal and Bangladesh constitutes of Region 5. The Indo-Gangetic Plains prime area means that the temperature varies from dry to mild climates. This means the city is having mild, humid, rainy summers and cold, dry winters. Monsoon rains which occur in this region most directly affect the climate.

Cuisine of Punjab is one of the most celebrated aspects of Punjabi culture. People of Punjab have a knack of experimenting successfully with their dishes. Be it vegetarian or non vegetarian dishes, there are so much varieties that even a person who lives in Punjab might not have tasted all. Punjabis are known to be fond of nutritious food and most of their delicacies are rich in flavor as well as are wholesome. The land is ideal for growing wheat and is called the "Granary of India" or "India's bread-basket". Though wheat varieties form their staple food, Punjabis do cook rice on special occasions. Food is mainly based upon wheat, masalas (spice), pure desi ghee, with liberal amounts of butter and cream. The practice of multi-cropping is quite common in Punjab which also grows sugarcane, bajra (pearl millet), jowar (great millet), barley, potatoes, vegetables and fruits among others. Cattle primarily used for agriculture and dairy farming in the region form the major source of dairy products starting from ghee, butter, clarified butter, curd, paneer (cottage cheese) to a wide variety of sweet dishes. Thus the staple foods grown locally including the dairy products form an integral part of the local diet. Non Vegetarian Punjab is home for mouth watering tandoori tikkas, kababs, roganjosh, fried fish dishes and much more. Curries can be made as dry or gravy preparation. There is hardly anyone in India who has not heard the name 'Makke Di Roti and Sarson Da Saag'. These are the two most famous dishes of Punjab. These dishes are exclusive to Punjab and among the many that have made a name for themselves outside the state. Dal Makhani, Shahi Panner, Aloo chole, Aloo Gobhi are the other few. The lavish use of ghee and vegetables in their dishes makes them quite heavy and nutritious. A tall glass full of cold Lassi (Churned Yogurt) is not only the favorite of Punjab people but you will find its admirers down south as well. Lassi can be salty as well as sweet but sweet Lassi is the more preferred one. Another famous sweet dish of Punjab is the Gajrela, a carrot pudding which is prepared by boiling milk sugar and grated carrot together. Cashews, almonds and raisins are added for extra flavor. Punjabis are also famous for their community food service called "Langar", where people of any caste or creed are fed with nutritious food without any cost. In rural Punjab, the community tandoor, dug in the ground, is a meeting place, just like the village well, for the women folk, who bring the kneaded atta (dough) and sometimes marinated meats to have them cooked while chit-chatting. Until a few years ago, this phenomenon existed in urban neighborhoods too. Even today, a few neighborhoods have a communal tandoor.

Haryanvi cuisine is like the people of Haryana - simple, earthy and inextricably linked to the land. In Haryana, the emphasis is on food that is wholesome, fresh and can be prepared easily. The 'Land of Rotis' is an apt title for Haryana, as people are fond of eating different kinds of rotis here. Wheat rotis are common and so are baajre ki roti. In earlier times, rotis would be made from a flour of wheat, gram and barley, a truly nutritious and healthy combination. The state is well known for its cattle wealth, so milk and milk products forms the major part of each food. People make butter and ghee at home and use these liberally in their daily diet. The refreshing Bathua-Ka-Raita (green leafy Bathua in delicately spiced yoghurt) and the lip-smacking Aloo-ki-Tikiyas (mashed, browned potatoes patties, stuffed with spicy lentils, smothered in sour tamarind chutney) are other favorites. Their cuisine is also inspired from the nearby states. As such, some dishes in Haryanvi Thali sound more like Rajasthani or Punjabi Thali. Haryanvi are traditionally vegetarians and take fresh vegetables are taken daily. Pethe ki subji is made on special occasions. The most relished dishes are Raabri and Bajre ki khichri with ghee or kadi. Teet ka achar is a pickle made of Kair tree. Some of the popular Haryana cuisines are Singri ki sabzi, Kachri ki Sabzi, Methi Gajar, Mixed Dal, Hara Dhania Cholia, Kadhi Pakora, Tamatar Chutney, Bathua Raita, Khichri, Mithe Chawal, Besan Masala Roti Makhan, Bhura Roti Ghee, Bajra Aloo Roti Makhan, Churma, Kheer and Malpuas.

There is no such thing as typical cuisines of Delhi. This is so because there is no specific identity of the city. This city is a whirlpool of different cultures and everyone contributes their significant little self to make a 'Dilliwala' exist. With time, people from different areas of India came and settled, making Delhi an assortment of sorts. Slowly and gradually, Delhi assumed some of the aspects of the identity of all the types of people living in it, making multiple identities for itself. As a result, even the traditional food of New Delhi has no distinctiveness. It comprises of South Indian food, Punjabi food, Gujarati food, Rajasthani food and so on. However, there are certain food items for which Delhi is quite famous. For example, Chandni Chowk area of the city boasts of the most delicious paranthas (a sort of bread). Infact, the entire area of Old Delhi is famous for the local Delhi cuisine. Then, there is the Bengali Market in New Delhi that is very popular for Chaat Papri, Golgappas, Sweets, etc. Some of the other popular road side eateries in Delhi include places like Paranthe wali gali, Annapoorna, Ghantewala, Bengali Market, Greater Kailash and Sunder Nagar are famous for entertaining their gastronomes with kababs, rotis chaat, bhelpuri, sweetmeats and biryani.

Awadhi cuisine is greatly influenced by Mughal cooking techniques similar to those of Persia, Kashmir, Punjab and Hyderabad which is famous for its royal food. The cuisine consists of both Vegetarian and Non – vegetarian delicacies. Mutton, paneer and spices like cardamom and saffron is highly used in these dishes. The lucknowi or the Awadhi cuisine is the result of the Nawabs who have ruled the city for more than ages. Dum Pukht, one of features of this cuisine, involves sealing the ingredients in large haandis placed over slow fire and allowing the ingredients to cook in their own juices and aromas. The richness of Awadhi cuisine lies not only in the variety of cuisine but its ingredients used in creating such a variety. The Chefs commonly called Babarchis in Awadh transformed the traditional dastarkhwan (laying of dinner on floor setting) the Persian word meaning a dining spread with elaborate dishes like Korma (braised meat in thick and rich gravy), Salan (a gravy dish of meat or vegetable), Keema (minced meat), Kababs (pounded meat fried or roasted over a charcoal fire), Bhujia (cooked vegetables), Daal (lintels), Pasanda (grilled ribbons of marinated tender meat, usually kid lamb or beef served as kabab or in rich gravy). Rice is cooked with meat in the form of a Pulao, Chulao (fried rice) or served plain. There would also be a variety of breads including Sheermaals, Parantha etc. Desserts comprised Gullati (rice pudding), Kheer (milk sweetened and boiled with whole rice to a thick consistency), Sheer Birinj, (a rich, sweet rice dish boiled in milk), Muzaaffar (vermicelli fried in ghee and garnished with saffron). The Awadhi menu changes with each season and is unique to the festivals that mark the month. The severity of winters is fought with rich food Paya (trotters) that are cooked overnight, over a slow fire and the 'shorba' (thick gravy) eaten with Kulcha (a flaky pastry type bread). The Awadhi cuisine is very traditional cuisine served from ages. It is very heavy cooked in Ghee and spices that are very rich and is prepared in dum pukht style.The Murg Mussallam is a typical example of Persian flavours merged with the Awadhi style of cooking. So is also the case with kababs. Originally, they were simply pieces of meat roasted over open fire, called boti kababs. Later, innovations were brought about in Awadh and the Shaami kababs, Galauti kababs, Kakori kababs, etc., were born out of innovations and improvisations here.

An abundant land provides for an abundant table. The nature and variety of dishes found in **Bengali** cooking are unique even in India. Fish cookery is one of its better –

known features and distinguishes it from the cooking of the landlocked regions. Bengal's countless rivers, ponds and lakes teem with many kinds of freshwater fish that closely resemble catfish, bass, shad or mullet. Bengalis prepare fish in innumerable ways – steamed or braised, or stewed with greens or other vegetables and with sauces that are mustard based or thickened with poppyseeds. You will not find these types of fish dishes elsewhere in India. Bengalis also excel in the cooking of vegetables. They prepare a variety of the imaginative dishes using the many types of vegetables that grow here year round. They can make ambrosial dishes out of the oftentimes rejected peels, stalks and leaves of vegetables. They use fuel – efficient methods, such as steaming fish or vegetables in a small covered bowl nestled at the top of the rice cooker. The use of spices for both fish and vegetable dishes is quite extensive and includes many combinations not found in other parts of India. Examples are the onion – flavored kalonji seeds and five – spice (a mixture of cumin, fennel, fenugreek, kalonji, and black mustard). The trump card card of Bengali cooking probably is the addition of this phoron, a combination of whole spices, fried and added at the start or finish of cooking as a flavouring special to each dish. Bengalis share a love of whole black mustard with South Indians, but the use of freshly ground mustard paste is unique to Bengal. All of India clamors for Bengali sweets. Although grains, beans and vegetables are used in preparing many deserts, as in other regions, the most delicious varieties are dairy – based and uniquely Bengali.

CHAPTER EIGHT

GLOSSARY of TERMS

- Ambal: A sour dish made either with several vegetables or with fish. (Bengal)
- Baghar: Tempering
- Bawarchis: Awadhi cooks
- Berani: Paratha stuffed with mashed dal
- Bhaja: Assorted fried items including vegetables and fish. (Bengal)
- Bhapa: Steamed (Bengali)
- Chhenchki: Tiny pieces of vegetables (Bengali)
- Daroga – e – Bawarchikhana: Incharge of Awadhi cuisine
- Dastarkhwan: Ceremonial dining spread where many people can sit together and have food.
- Dhaba: Road side eateries.
- Dhoka: Steamed balls of dal in a salan
- Dum dena: Cooked in sealed pot. (Awadhi)
- Galka: Sweet sour chutney made from raw mangoes.
- Ganga – Jamuni tehzeeb: Hindu Muslim unity – phrase
- Ghanto: Mixture of vegetables and dal (Bengali dish)
- Gupchup: Golgappa, Panipuri,
- Haleem: Khichri made of dals, wheat and meat

- Hamam dista: It is a pair of tools used to crush, grind, and mix solid substances or masalas. It is usually made of iron but can also be made of marble stone, wood, bamboo, iron, steel, brass and basalt.
- Hatha: Ladle in Bengali
- Havan: Lighting of Holi fire of Hindus.
- Kal – baisakhi: Hot winds in Bengal
- Kandi: The name given to semi-hilly area in Punjab.
- Kanhaar: Person who serve water in Awadhi
- Kanjee: Fermented carrot and mustard paste drink, served in earthen ware —matka
- Kathi Rolls: Kati roll is a street-food dish originating from Kolkata, India. In its original form, it is a skewer-roasted kebab wrapped in paratha bread; although over the years many variants have evolved all of which now go under the generic name of kati roll. Today, mostly any wrap containing a filling enfolded in an Indian flatbread (roti) is called a kati roll.
- Khoncha: It is a flat metal spoon used for stir frying or sautéing the ingredients.
- Khunti: Spatula in Bengali.
- Langar: Community dining hall organized by the Punjabis.
- Laute paute: Gram flour pancakes—rolled, sliced, and served in a salan
- Loab: Oil floating on top of gravies in Awadhi cuisine.
- Masalchi: Person who grinds masalas in Awadhi cuisine
- Mehrin: Person who cleans utensils in Awadhi cuisine
- Moin: Rubbing together fat and flour.
- Moori: Puffed rice (Bengali)
- Multani tikka: Crispy ajwain flavored paneer and onion tikka, served with tandoor kebab masala.

- Musallam: Marinated chicken/mutton/vegetable
- Muzzaffar: Sewiyaan in Awadhi
- Nafasat: Refinement
- Nanfus: Awadhi naan – roti makers
- Naru: Sweet made from grated coconut and jagary. (Bengal)
- Nazaakat: Delicateness
- Nimona: Crushed green peas curry.(Awadhi)
- Noon chai: Kashmiri tea making pink colored tea.
- Pakhal: One day old fermented rice (Odisha)
- Panch phoron: A Bengali combination of cumin seeds, Fennel, mustard seeds, methi seeds and onion seeds.
- Pangat: One family compiled of all of humanity, regardless of caste, color, or creed, sitting together cross legged in lines, forming rows without discrimination or consideration of rank or position.
- Paya: Paya is an Urdu word that denotes the trotter or foot. This recipe of Paya curry has sheep's trotters, cooked in a luscious tomato- onion curry. This is a famous Mughlai dish of Northern India.
- Paye: Stewed trotters of goat.
- Pitha: Pancake (Bengal)
- Rakhabdar: Person involved in presentation and service of Awadhi food
- Rara gosht: A rich heavy and thick mutton preparation in which mutton boti and mutton mince is cooked together with onion and masalas till done.
- Rau di kheer: A dessert made of sugarcane juice and rice.
- Rumaali: Paper thin roti
- Sangat: The ennobling influence of people, who aspire to truthful living, and congregate with like-minded company for the purpose of uttering the name of one

God in the presence of the Guru Granth.
- Shakramba: Sweet n sour dessert made of mango.
- Shikanji: Chilled drink made of chili water, lemon juice, salt, sugar black salt powder and black pepper powder
- Taftan: Leavened bread.(Awadhi)
- Tikiyas: Mashed, fried browned potatoes patties, stuffed with spicy lentils, smothered in sour tamarind chutney.
- Yagna: A ritual sacrifice with a specific objective
- Zarda: Sweet rice (Awadhi)

The Author

Meet the remarkable **Dr. Anshumali Pandey**, a living testament to excellence in education, hospitality, tourism, and the fascinating world of tribal food. A true polymath, he effortlessly wears the hats of a seasoned educator, esteemed chef, celebrated author, meticulous business auditor, and adventurous culinary traveller.

With a focus on higher education, office administration, HR, labour laws, audit, procurement, and tender processes, Dr. Pandey has gained prominence as a leading hospitality educator, holding a distinguished PhD in the field of Management.

Fuelling his passion for tribal food, tourism, and village exploration, he has delved deep into extensive research, leading to numerous illuminating research papers and publications. Notably, the Ministry of Tourism, Government of India, recognized his expertise and contributions, bestowing upon him a National Appreciation certificate and a cherished memento in 2018.

Drawing from a rich experience spanning over 29 years in the professional realm, Dr. Anshumali Pandey has honed the art of precise and compelling writing. This has resulted in an impressive collection of 130 publications, comprising 90 enlightening books and captivating short stories. His literary repertoire covers a wide spectrum, ranging from culinary expertise to HR mastery, from nurturing young minds through children's books to exploring the realms of spirituality.

Residing with his family in the picturesque Western Indian tribal belt of the union territory of Dadra & Nagar Haveli for more than two decades, Dr. Pandey has wholeheartedly dedicated his time to understanding and aiding the tribal and rural communities of the region. His writings not only showcase his immense expertise but also reflect his profound knowledge of diverse subjects he has thoughtfully chosen for his books.

A true champion of the hospitality sector, Dr. Anshumali Pandey's multifaceted prowess has established him as a reputable and revered name in the industry. His boundless passion and unwavering commitment make him an inspiring figure for aspiring professionals across various fields.

Books written by the Author are –

1. Theory of Indian Cookery (2 Editions Printed)
2. Beauty and Irony of Silvassa Tourism
3. A Short Indian Food Story

4. Be Your Own Guide to Indian Cuisine
5. Cookery Fundamentals
6. History of Indian Food (2 Editions Printed)
7. The Great Indian Story Book for Children
8. Personal Budget: Easy Work Book
9. Online Classes Log Book
10. Dictionary Making Work Book for School Children
11. The Lazy Bed
12. Hindu Dharm (हिन्दू धर्म) (In Hindi Language)
13. Where is my coffee?
14. Your First Job is Never your Last (Volume 1)
15. You are Almost There (Quick Fix Resume and Interview Hacks)
16. Working for the Enemy? - A lesson in Career Management
17. Public Speaking for the Young
18. A Date With Coffee
19. How to be The Best Hotel Front Office Employee
20. Diploma in Food Production, The complete Syllabus
21. Diploma in F&B Service, The Complete Syllabus
22. Diploma in Front Office, The Complete Syllabus
23. The Time to Speak is Now
24. Munshi Premchand (Short Stories in English)
25. The Housekeeping Department, Text Book
26. Hitchhiker's Guide to Trekking in Uttarakhand
27. Uttarakhand, A divine Land for a Reason
28. Bachhon ke liye rochak kahaniyan (बच्चों के लिए रोचक कहानियाँ) (In Hindi Language)
29. Basic Communication Skills of English
30. The Basic Office Organisation Book for Start-ups
31. Hospitality HRM
32. Hospitality Marketing

33. Bakery Ingredients and Tools
34. Human Resource Management for Indian Professionals
35. The process of LAWFULLY operating a Hospitality business in India
36. Indian Classical Sweets: History, Tradition and Recipes
37. History of India's Himalayan Cuisine: Classical Cookery of Kashmir, Laddakh, Jammu, Himachal, Lahaul, Spiti, Garhwal, Kumaon.
38. Vindu: Andhra Cuisine (Part 1 of South Indian Trilogy)
39. Saappadu: Tamil Cuisine (Part 2 of South Indian Trilogy)
40. Sadya: Malayali Cuisine (Part 3 of South Indian Trilogy)
41. South Indian Cuisine - The Researcher's Guide Book
42. The Ramayana for Children and other short stories from Indian Mythology
43. Legends of the Tribal Shiva
44. Third Generation Children's Story Book
45. It's Elementary: The Top Nine Adventures from the memoirs of Dr John H Watson (2 Editions Printed)
46. UNITY IN DIVERSITY, The foundation of Indian Tourism
47. The Thar Express: Culinary History of Rajasthan and Gujarat
48. Basics of Computerized Accounting
49. Impact (Impact of Globalization on Indian Social Life)
50. Vishnu – The Lord of Amazing Incarnations
51. Being a Mahatma in the Freedom Struggle
52. The Culinary Journey of Purvanchal: Lucknow to Patna
53. Culinary History of the Gangetic Plains
54. Indian Culinary Secrets
55. The Story of Jain and Parsi Food
56. The Great Indian Pilgrimage Tourism
57. Introduction to Tourism Studies – Text Book

58. Bread and Rolls (2 Editions Printed)
59. Diploma in Digital Marketing the Complete Syllabus
60. The Theory of Sweetened Bakery Foods
61. Campus Placement Guide for Management Trainee in Leading Hotels
62. Diploma in Housekeeping Management, the Complete Syllabus
63. Jokes and Stories for Kids
64. Demigods of India
65. Practical Cookery Guide Book for Parents and School Teachers
66. Introduction to Cookery for Elementary School Children (Kindle)
67. The Fearless Entrepreneur (Being your own Boss)
68. Culinary Heritage of Bengal's Widow Culture
69. Journey into the Mythological Wisdom of Vedas & Puranas
70. From Stigma to Strength: The Legacy of Bengal's Widowhood
71. HAKKA: Discovering a Vibrant Community in India
72. The Indo Chinese Pot Boiler
73. Bombay Daak: *Discovering the Kolis of the Seven Islands*
74. Speak Your Mind: A Guide to Clear and Impactful Communication
75. Urbanization And Rural Dynamics In India
76. Short Stories from the Animal Kingdom
77. The Short Story Book for Children - Morals and Humour
78. Advance Tourism Studies
79. Indian Knowledge Systems
80. The Geography of India: A Comprehensive Text Book and Guide
81. The Alpha Book of Researches Volume I
82. Introduction to Management

83. Organizational Behaviour
84. Principles of Management and Organizational Behaviour
85. Advanced studies in Indian Knowledge Systems
86. MCQ Companion on Indian Knowledge Systems
87. Rivers of Justice
88. Indian Economy MCQs: 1800 Questions with answer Key for UGC NET, UPSC & Competitive Exams
89. Fundamentals of the Indian and Global Business Environment
90. Gangotri to Gangasagar: A Culinary Journey

Google me for latest updates: Dr Anshumali Pandey
https://notionpress.com/author/337004
Connect with me: anshumali.pandey@gmail.com

Please scan this QR code on your phone to know more about the latest and complete works of Dr Anshumali Pandey